# Behind The Mask Of Adolescent Satanism

## by Joyce Mercer

Minneapolis, Minnesota

Acknowledgments: I am grateful to many friends across the duration of this writing enterprise: The Pastoral Care staff at Riverside Medical Center and especially my colleagues Dave Berg and LaDonna Benes in adolescent dependency; to Dr. Mary Farrell Bednarowski of United Theological Seminary in the Twin Cities, who carefully read parts of the manuscript and offered helpful suggestions; the helpful folks at Deaconess Press; the Befriender Ministers at Mayflower church in Minneapolis; and of course to my partner in marriage, Larry Golemon, who in spite of becoming something of a "book widower" during this writing, loves teenagers and me, too.

No part of this book may be used or reproduced in any manner whatsoever without written permission except in the case of brief quotations embodied in critical articles and reviews. For information address DEACONESS PRESS, 2450 Riverside Avenue South, Minneapolis, MN 55454.

First published September, 1991.
Copyright © 1991 by Joyce Mercer. All rights reserved.
Printed in the United States of America.

96 95 94 93 92    5 4 3 2

Avon Books has granted permission to use extended quotations from the books: *The Satanic Bible*, by Anton LaVey, Copyright 1969 by Anton LaVey, and from *The Satanic Rituals*, by Anton LaVey, Copyright 1972 by Anton LaVey.

Cover design by Ned Skubic

ISBN 0-925190-22-5
Library of Congress Catalog Card Number 91-072991

Editor's Note: DEACONESS PRESS publishes many books and pamphlets related to the subjects of chemical dependency and mental health. These publications do not necessarily reflect the philosophies of behavioral health programs provided by Fairview, nor any 12-Step Program or any other behavioral health program.

# Contents

To young people risking recovery.

# Foreword

Satanism is much feared and little understood. When mixed with the mysteries of adolescence, the apprehensions of their parents and the risks inherent in growing up, it has spawned distortion, panic and destruction.

Popular writings often add to the confusion. Their portrayals of satanic rituals and analyses of satanic beliefs are one-dimensional, lack perspective and in many cases they are sensational.

Joyce Mercer understands teenagers. She knows the risks and choices many kids are faced with as they grow up in today's culture. She has taken the time and care to explore the multi-dimensional nature of satanism among kids. The result is a clearly-written, carefully-crafted, in-depth exploration of one of the least understood and most feared elements of American society.

Her distinction between satanism as a "religious" experience versus satanism as a screen for projected adolescent rebellion, alienation and disenfranchisement is critical for anyone seeking to understand adolescent satanism. Joyce leads the reader into the theological, religious, sociological, psychological and methodological considerations necessary for a wise and compassionate response.

The links Joyce makes between adolescent development and satanism are persuasive and empowering. Anyone who knows adolescent development is able to undersand the allure that satanism has for teenagers at risk.

Perhaps the greatest value of this work is the combination of practical approaches for a balanced response to teens involved in satanism. Joyce provides a road map for developing healthy adolescent spirituality that both respects teenage experiences *and* calls teens to grow into a hopeful future.

Roland D. Martinson

Professor of Pastoral Care
Luther Northwestern Theological Seminary
St. Paul, Minnesota

# INTRODUCTION

"Chaplain, we have a young man on our treatment unit who is talking about his involvement in a satanic cult. Will you see him?"

"One of our new outpatient clients says that Satan is his Higher Power. Will you please talk with the staff about some ways to deal with this?"

"My daughter is acting really strange lately and I'm worried. I found some satanic symbols on her notebook, and a neighbor who goes to her school told me that she hangs around with a group who performs satanic rituals. I'm really scared. What's this satanic stuff all about?"

As a chaplain for an adolescent chemical dependency treatment program, my own interest in adolescent Satan worship began out of the practical need to respond to requests such as these. Along with other staff in the program, I was taken aback by the power such an identification had among other youth in the treatment community. Satanism also appeared to bring out strong reactions from the staff, who found difficulty locating good informed sources about dealing with satanic teens. I was also surprised by the increasing frequency with which young people in treatment identified themselves as "satanic" or "Satan worshipers."

Judging from news reports about satanic activity in Texas, Minnesota, Connecticut and California, teen participation in satanic groups appears to be on the rise nationwide. Counselors, clinicians, clergy and parents alike wonder how best to understand and respond. Meanwhile, the media provides a continual backdrop for the confusion and fear surrounding adolescent satanism with stories of secret rituals and links between Satan worship and crimes of vandalism and murder. Speakers and workshops abound, complete with gory tales of mutilation and photographs carefully chosen for their shock value. This book cuts through the sensationalism surrounding adolescent Satan worship by providing resources for parents and professionals to help them understand and respond to adolescents connected with satanism.

Several of the chapters directly concern the practice of satanism, its various forms, and perspectives about satanism as we see it in our society. Chapter 2, "Exploring the Power Pact," focuses on the phenomenon of *adolescent* satanism. Adolescent satanism looks different than other expressions of satanic activity, and its distinctive features are spelled out throughout the book. Chapter 5, "The Idea of the Devil," explores the various sources for a teenager's concept of Satan. Parents and professionals working with teens need to recognize that there is not a single concept all teens have in mind when they talk about satanism. What adolescents mean when they refer to "Satan" is a composite picture drawn from many sources. To understand their perspectives—as well as our own—it is important to look at various sources and meanings within the idea of Satan.

Chapter 3 on adolescent development might appear to have little or nothing to do with the subject at hand. This chapter rarely mentions satanism. It focuses upon the internal, developmental experience of adolescents as they journey from childhood toward adulthood. The elements that contribute to teen attraction to satanism cannot be understood in a vacuum or separate from the other realities taking place in a teen's life. While Chapter 2 considers external factors influencing teens, Chapter 3 builds a foundation for understanding the internal psychological factors of adolescence. Adolescent satanism cannot be understood apart from such a perspective. Consequently, I spend a significant amount of time on the connection between adolescent developmental issues and satanism. The chapter on adolescent development provides some necessary background for readers not accustomed to thinking about teens in developmental terms.

The final two chapters move toward issues of recovery, change, and health. The first of these chapters deals with assessing the need for help when a young person appears to be involved with satanism, and looks at some helpful responses adults can offer. The final chapter asks, "What is healthy adolescent spirituality?" and considers some ways adults can support teens in the development of healthy spirituality.

Teen satanism arises to fill a void, to meet unfulfilled needs of young people. This book argues that an important need fulfilled by teen satanism concerns power. Young people also seek ways to express the great, intangible aspects of life with which they come into contact—forces of love and hatred, a greater sense of purpose or meaning, devotion to a cause or ideal, questions of ethics and values, the ability to identify with other people and feel compassion, and a sense of connection or "community." These are spiritual concerns of young people.

When healthy, positive spirituality is absent, young people will seek other ways to address their spiritual needs. For some teens, satanism fulfills the need to give symbolic expression to the intangible, cosmic, or even "supernatural" aspects of life. The perspectives on healthy adolescent spirituality given in Chapter 5 arise out of a desire to help parents and professionals understand the spiritual needs of teens, so that these adults can encourage healthy spiritual growth.

Frequently when I talk with people about adolescent satanic practices, I am asked whether I believe in the Devil, or what I believe about Satan. Although my personal beliefs are irrelevant to the issue, I appreciate the desire on the part of questioners to know the world view that informs my thinking. I am a Presbyterian minister, a clinical social worker, and a human being who has seen and experienced some small part of evil. I was born into a generation that knows possibilities of events like the Nazi Holocaust, the nuclear bombing of Hiroshima, or child sexual abuse.

But those who have shaped much of my perspective on adolescent satanism are young people in chemical dependency treatment. As they come to terms with a spirituality that supports their recovery, many of these young people have had the courage to address their participation in satanic groups. Their belief in Satan, and the dynamics that compel them to express themselves through involvement in satanic groups, is the subject of this book. The individual names of the adolescents are altered. But all of the examples and conversations come from real situations.

Joyce Ann Mercer
Summer, 1991
Minneapolis, Minnesota

# Chapter 1

## SATANISM: WHAT IS IT?

*"Worship the Devil, Satan's power will free you.*
*Evil within will allow you to be you."*
—from a poem by a 16-year-old female

"A glow of new light is borne out of the night and Lucifer is risen, once more to proclaim: 'This is the age of Satan! Satan rules the Earth!...The *flesh* prevaileth and a great Church shall be builded, consecrated in its name...Hail Satan"—Anton Szandor LaVey, *The Satanic Bible.* [1]

Is satanism a religion? A cult? A movement? The San Francisco telephone book classifies the Church of Satan alongside Catholic, Baptist, Presbyterian, and other Christian groups as a church. The media frequently identify adolescent satanism as a cult, referring to acts of vandalism or other crimes linked with satanists as "cult crimes." A fundamentalist clergy person recently called satanism "a dark spiritual movement in the cosmic battle for our children's souls." Just what is adolescent satanism? One way to address these questions is to look at the Church of Satan, with its similarities and differences to adolescent satanic practices.

1

## The Emergence of Satanism In America

A number of new religious groups found their way onto the American landscape during the late 1960s and early 1970s—including the Church of Satan. Some of these new religions, such as Hare Krishna and the Unification Church originated in the Eastern religious traditions of Asia. Others, like the Church of Scientology/Dianetics and *est* were propelled into popularity by the growing encounter group/human relations movement. Such new religious movements share in common with the Church of Satan their location outside the mainstream of the American religious establishment. The social upheaval of the time was marked by questioning, mistrust, and protest against established religious and governmental institutions. This turmoil provided a fertile ground for the emergence of new religious movements. The Church of Satan is distinct in that it alone centers its symbolism and ideology around the figure who is the very antithesis of that mainstream religious establishment—Satan.

## Anton S. LaVey and The Church of Satan

Adolescents involved in satanic groups are not part of the Church of Satan. Yet, they frequently utilize two books written by its founder, Anton Szander LaVey, in their satanic activity and worship: *The Satanic Bible* and *The Satanic Rituals*. LaVey began the Church of Satan in California in 1966 as an antidote to what he considered the primary agenda of the Christian church—the denial of sexuality and intellect. LaVey is a colorful figure with an equally colorful background that includes work in a California police lab, a stint as a carnival and circus worker, animal trainer, and a minor film career.

On April 30, 1966, LaVey shaved his head and declared the beginning of a new era, heralding the reign of Satan. Early in its

2

existence the Church of Satan attained considerable visibility, with press coverage of events such as a satanic funeral held for a Navy man killed in an accident at the Treasure Island Naval Base. LaVey played the role of Satan in the movie *Rosemary's Baby*, a film achieving widespread popularity with its story of a woman impregnated by the Devil. So the Church of Satan had a certain degree of visibility and notoriety from the outset.

At the height of its popularity in the 1970's, the Church of Satan claimed 10,000 members, with groups called "grottos" forming in several major cities across the country. Social science researchers suggest that this number is inflated, and probably has never risen above 2,000 people who pay the lifetime membership fee of $100. J. Gordon Melton, a specialist in American religions who researches new cults and new religious groups, reports that in 1974, the Church of Satan experienced a major upheaval in its membership when a majority left the church to found other satanic groups. Despite a reported upsurge in membership in the mid-1980s, Melton notes that in 1985 the Church of Satan only mailed out approximately 2,000 copies of its newsletter, *The Cloven Hoof.* [2]

Contrary to belief, the Church of Satan is not an aggressive "cult" making mass converts of thousands of unsuspecting young people who are deceptively lulled into membership. Instead the Church of Satan appears to be a small, fairly localized group which rarely includes adolescent membership. Its significance for adolescent Satan worship may be seen in the way teens find the ideology of the Church of Satan attractive, and loosely pattern many of their practices after those described in the writings of Anton LaVey.

## What the Church of Satan Believes

The basic premise of the Church of Satan is that the Christian church exists to foster sexual repression, self-denial and repression of the intellect. Such criticisms are neither uncommon nor unique to LaVey. Other groups, including groups from within Christianity, also make such charges. However, LaVey's intention was to establish an openly practicing group that would be the very antithesis of the Christian church as he understood it. And so LaVey used the language of the church, and even co-opted its scriptures, to give shape to his Church of Satan.

## Self-Elevation

A look at *The Satanic Bible*, written after the Church of Satan began in 1966, reveals several major beliefs. First, the focus of satanic belief is not so much Satan or the "person" of the Devil, as much as the Self. LaVey's satanism believes in the supremacy of the self, expressed in self-gratification, self-indulgence, and self-aggrandizement. Church of Satan members distinguish themselves from practitioners of so-called "white magic," and witches who practice ancient fertility/nature rituals because witches revere nature while "Satanists worship none but themselves." [3] Instead of being a figure to be worshipped, Satan represents certain ideas LaVey views as central in human existence. These include "the belief that humans are simply another animal among all the animals..." and therefore act on instinct, the notion that acting out of vengeance is more natural than kindness because few people truly deserve kindness, and the idea that Satan represents "the so-called sins which lead to physical and mental gratification." [4] In other words, it is not so much the *character* of Satan, as what LaVey believes Satan to *represent* in terms of self-glorification that forms the core of beliefs for the Church of Satan. Common in the writings of LaVey are statements suggesting that each person determines the "rules" for himself or herself. One section in *The Satanic Bible* bears the subtitle, "The God You Save May Be Yourself." LaVey considers the strongest human instinct to be self-preservation, and views attempts by Jewish and Christian groups to elevate concern for others as a self-repressive effort that goes against what is most basic to the human being: "Hate your enemies with a whole heart, and if a man smite you on one cheek, *smash* him on the other!' Smite him hip and thigh, for self-preservation is the highest law!" Fittingly, the most important holiday observed by members of the Satanic Church is their own birthday, as an expression of the ideology of "self above all else."

## The Nine Satanic Statements

The focus upon self-gratification rather than elevation and worship of a supernatural being known as Satan is central to understanding the Church of Satan. This is what young people find so appealing about satanism. It is best illustrated in an examination of the Nine Satanic Statements, one of several passages in *The Satanic Bible* providing readers with a brief encapsulation of the church's beliefs:

1. Satan represents indulgence, instead of abstinence!
2. Satan represents vital existence, instead of spiritual pipe dreams!
3. Satan represents undefiled wisdom, instead of hypocritical self-deceit!
4. Satan represents kindness to those who deserve it, instead of love wasted on ingrates!
5. Satan represents vengeance, instead of turning the other cheek!
6. Satan represents responsibility to the responsible, instead of concern for psychic vampires!
7. Satan represents man as just another animal, sometimes

better, more often worse than those that walk on all
fours, who, because of his "divine spiritual and intellec–
tual development," has become the most vicious animal
of all!
8. Satan represents all of the so-called sins, as they all
lead to physical, mental or emotional gratification!
9. Satan has been the best friend the church has ever
had, as he has kept it in business all these years! [5]

The focus of these nine statements is two-fold. First, they
emphasize satanic ideology as existing in opposition to Christian
beliefs. And second, they identify Satan in terms of a self-elevating
ideology rather than a personal or evil being.

There is an obvious oppositional quality to each statement.
Most of the statements express what Satan represents in terms of
the opposite of what the Christian church represents. So, the
indulgence of satanism is contrasted with the abstinence he sees
the church promoting; a focus on reality ("vital existence" and
"undefiled wisdom") is contrasted with denial ("pipe dreams" and
"hypocritical self-deceit"). It is an intentional contrast, with an
equally intentional borrowing of the language and vocabulary of
Christian tradition to express satanic thoughts—hence the very
term satanic *"church."*

In contrast to popular understandings of satanism, there is little
attention devoted to Satan as a specific being, or even evil. Even
when Satan is identified, as in the above Nine Satanic Statements,
what is said usually takes the shape of a metaphor—Satan as the
symbol for a belief about self-supremacy.

### Sexual Gratification

If the first principle of the Church of Satan is exalting the self
above all else, a closely related second principle is its promotion

of sexual gratification and indulgence. One would expect this to be the case in a group founded for the purpose of overcoming sexual repression. After self-preservation, according to LaVey, sex is the strongest human instinct. This emphasis on "sexual gratification" finds expression in the rituals LaVey developed in a book entitled *The Satanic Rituals*, as well as in the ideological underpinnings of satanic beliefs.

For example, in his discussion of the "requirements for performance of the Black Mass," LaVey includes the following details on how to properly carry out the ceremony:

> The woman who serves as the altar lies on the platform with her body at right angles to its length, her knees at its edge and widely parted. A pillow supports her head. Her arms are outstretched crosswise and each hand grasps a candle-holder containing a black candle. When the celebrant is at the altar, he stands between the woman's knees. [6]

These instructions presume an understanding from *The Satanic Bible* that in satanic rituals the altar is formed by a nude woman "because woman is the natural passive receptor and represents the earth mother." LaVey also instructs followers on the proper clothing to be worn for satanic ritual. Males are to wear black robes, while females are to clothe themselves in "garments which are sexually suggestive"—unless they are older women, in which case they may wear all black clothing. LaVey does not address the issue of "sexual indulgence" for women. The emphasis rests completely on male sexual pleasure. LaVey seems to believe that since women are "natural passive receptors" they experience their gratification through sexually suggestive clothing and seductive acts towards men. One researcher, Randall Alfred, calls LaVey's second published book, *The Compleat Witch*, "essentially a seduction manual for witches" which emerged from a workshop LaVey taught women in the late 1960's. [7] Many of the rituals employ the use of a "phallus, for which any phallic symbol will suffice."

Satanic ideology emphasizes sexual gratification from the perspective of its founder. The result is a message that, in the name of sexual freedom and anti-repression, encourages objectification of persons—especially women. It also promotes a viewpoint that the highest value in sexual intimacy is one's own good feelings, apart from other aspects of intimacy such as care for the partner, or responsibility in sexual behavior. Such ideology can appear very attractive and freeing to some adolescents as we will see later.

### Magic and Ritual

In a general discussion about the use of magic, *The Satanic Bible* defines magic as "the change in situations or events in accordance with one's will, which would, using normally accepted methods, be unchangeable."[8] Lesser magic is the everyday, ordinary manipulation of one's environment to accomplish some purpose. Greater magic brings about change, according to LaVey, through the performance of a ritual.

There are three types of rituals. The first is a "sex ritual" "to create desire on the part of the person whom you desire, or to summon a sex partner to fulfill your desires."[9] Church of Satan members can attend classes to learn how to ceremonially cast spells for this purpose. The second type of ritual is a "compassion, or sentiment ritual." It helps the self or others. LaVey carefully reminds readers, however, that charity begins at home—a warning against what he considers false altruism or hypocritical charity. The third type of ritual is a "destruction ritual. This is a ceremony used for anger, annoyance, disdain, contempt, or just plain hate."[10]

LaVey says he employed the destruction ritual to bring about the death of actress Jayne Mansfield, a follower of LaVey. LaVey claims responsibility for her death because he directed the ritual toward Sam Brody, Mansfield's manager, which inadvertently affected her. Although *The Satanic Bible*, and LaVey when interviewed, explicitly state that hurting people or animals is not condoned, there are constant references to "eliminating persons who get in the way" or are "obnoxious." This apparent contradiction is especially visible in *The Eleven Satanic Rules of the Earth*. Taken from a recent interview with Anton LaVey, these statements provide a thumbnail sketch of the underlying ideology of the Church of Satan:

### The Eleven Satanic Rules of the Earth

1. Do not give opinions or advice unless you are asked.
2. Do not tell your troubles to others unless you are sure they want to hear them.
3. When in another's lair, show him respect or else do not go there.
4. If a guest in your lair annoys you, treat him cruelly and without mercy.
5. Do not make sexual advances unless you are given the mating signal.
6. Do not take that which does not belong to you unless it is a burden to the other person and he cries out to be relieved.
7. Acknowledge the power of magic if you have employed it successfully to obtain your desires. If you deny the power of magic after having called upon it with success, you will lose all you have obtained.
8. Do not complain about anything to which you need not subject yourself.

9. Do not harm little children.
10. Do not kill non-human animals unless attacked, or for your food.
11. When walking in open territory, bother no one. If someone bothers you, ask him to stop. If he does not stop, destroy him. [11]

These statements act as a "code of ethics," a guide for behavior. We will return to them later to consider their appeal to adolescents. Concerning the issue of criminal behavior and the Church of Satan, these statements present multiple contradictions. On the one hand, some of them appear to urge respect for others and to counsel a person not to behave in a way that is burdensome to others: "Do not give opinions or advice unless you are asked." On the other hand, they authorize aggressive actions: "If a guest in your lair annoys you, treat him cruelly and without mercy."

Despite the contradictions inherent in these statements (especially 9 - 11), LaVey contends that his rituals do not involve criminal activity, human or animal sacrifice. And many criminologists who follow the activity of the Church of Satan contend that there is no evidence linking the church with criminal involvement. The violence and destruction associated with satanism appears to have come from other groups of satanists who are not a part of LaVey's Church of Satan.

In addition to the rituals mentioned above, a number of ceremonies are described in *The Satanic Rituals*, complete with instructions about the type of music to be used, appropriate clothing, and who should participate. The book includes "The Black Mass" and a "Satanic Baptism" ceremony. These ceremonies have a distinctive style of mocking Christian ritual.

## Conclusions About the Church of Satan

What does all this information about the Church of Satan mean? First and foremost, it is important to evaluate information about the Church of Satan within its social and cultural context. The Church of Satan emerged in a time when many new movements opposing "the establishment" came into being. It was a time to challenge traditional institutions and centers of meaning. And so it should not be surprising to find the emergence of the Church of Satan, a religious group which defined itself as the very opposite of what it saw as most despicable in established, mainline religions.

Second, the Church of Satan itself has been a rather small, harmless and low-key operation. Most of the attention it has received, after the initial media interest of the early 1970's died down, occurs when someone outside the Church of Satan, often someone from the Religious Right or of a fundamentalist Christian group, gets worked up and goes on a public campaign against it.

And finally, another perspective by which to evaluate the significance and seriousness of the Church of Satan is to look at the validity of the premises upon which its ideology rests. The Church of Satan is an expression of institutionalized satanism based upon opposition to its founder's beliefs about Christianity. There does seem to be a certain internal logic to satanism, if one grants the basic premises of LaVey that Christianity is inherently anti-sexual and anti-intellectual. The Church of Satan's solution to these perceived problems in Christianity is to create a "theology" that exists as the very antithesis to (LaVey's beliefs about) Christianity.

Everyone can name examples of situations, historic or current, in which Jewish and Christian theologies have been misinterpreted and used repressively. The fact that such examples occur does not mean that repression is the *goal* of those faith systems. If some people grow obese from eating, this does not mean that the primary purpose of ingesting food is to get fat. The Church of

Satan's ideology depends upon acceptance of its extremely narrow interpretation of Christian beliefs.

What is serious and significant about the Church of Satan is not what the church itself espouses, but what certain other groups intrigued by its ideology are doing in the name of satanism. Adolescent satanists are one such group.

## What About Teenagers?

So far, we have considered characteristics and beliefs of the Church of Satan. This is not the group referred to when discussing adolescent Satan worship. J. Gordon Melton identifies two groups of satanists beyond the Church of Satan and its splinter groups, which he describes as "a small, closed group consisting primarily of either (1) young teenagers experimenting with the occult and/ or drugs, or (2) sociopaths and psychopaths." [12] Neither is a part of the organization headed by Anton LaVey.

In the case of "sociopaths and psychopaths," Melton suggests that such groups come and go quickly, as they release through their activity whatever psychopathic urge led to the group's formation in the first place. But what about teenagers? What is their link to satanism? A quick sketch of adolescent satanism shows several characteristics common to these groups:

1. They consist of individuals or small groups of teenagers which exist independently of one another and are not connected to any central structure or organization.

2. The groups of adolescents practicing satanism generally are not long-lived. They may be together for several months or only a few hours before disbanding.

3. There is no common belief system or ideology among the adolescents practicing satanism, nor a widespread common ritual practice. Common symbols and elements may be seen across groups, but a distinctive aspect of adolescent satanism is that the individuals and groups tend to make it up as they go along.

4. Drug use is common among adolescent satanists.

5. Teenagers involved in satanic groups often utilize *The Satanic Bible* and *The Satanic Rituals*, along with other similar writings, to devise their practices or give credibility to their groups. Their own imaginations and images of satanic or occult activity from popular culture constitute a major source for their understanding of satanism.

6. Many adolescents express an interest in the occult or in satanism. A group of adolescent satanists may have individuals at varying levels of involvement.

There is one characteristic of adolescent satanism not yet mentioned. It does not fit neatly into a list. Yet it is perhaps the most important of all. It has to do with why adolescents find satanism attractive, why they get involved in groups practicing self-styled satanic rituals, and why they are so interested in its symbolism.

Teenagers involved in satanism are there because it meets some need for them. And one primary need met by their involvement with satanic writings or a satanic group is the need for power. How does satanism give them power? What kind of power do they seek? Who do they gain power over? Why satanism and not something else as a way to achieve power? Adolescent satanism is a kind of power pact.

## Chapter 2

## EXPLORING THE POWER PACT

A young man rushes home from school, goes up to his room and locks the door. He pulls out a small box from under his bed—a box carefully hidden by a pile of clothes and his baseball glove. He takes out a book and begins to read, relaxing on the bed. He smiles as fantasies run through his head—fantasies of getting back at his parents, teachers who get on his nerves, and people who have snubbed him. He reads for a while longer, returns the book to its hiding place, and goes downstairs to the kitchen for a snack as his parents arrive home from work. They exchange small talk about their day, and the boy answers the telephone. His parents begin to discuss whether they should delay dinner for another one of his phone calls. He forgets all about the book and his fantasies as he talks with his friend for the next half-hour. The book hidden under his bed is *The Satanic Bible*.

§

Elsewhere, a teenage girl sits in fear as she watches a couple of her peers kill a stray cat and take blood from its neck. Some of the blood is collected in a small cup that will become a "chalice" in their ritual. The girl is there out of curiosity, because they had told her they worshipped Satan, and it sounded exciting. But this situation feels different. She starts to tell her friends that she wants to go home. The words stick in her throat as she wonders what they will think of her if she leaves now.

One of her peers hands her a joint of marijuana.

"What's the matter," he says, "scared?"

"No," she replies. "I just didn't know you were going to kill the cat."

"If you can't handle it..."

"I can handle it." She smokes some of the marijuana and begins to feel the high. "Sure, I can handle anything."

They get together a few more times, but drug use is the real focus. Satan worship gives them the excuse to get together to use. Soon they no longer need the excuse, and so satanic rituals and language drops out of sight altogether.

§

Shawn attends a large urban high school. It is easy to get lost there, to be another face in the crowd—especially because Shawn has just transferred to the school after his family moved from a small town. He is not an outstanding student, nor is he an athlete. He has a hard time finding a group he can fit into, until mid-year, when he meets Kevin and John.

Kevin and John seem a lot like Shawn. The three of them begin to stick together. One day, as a joke, one of them says out loud that the three of them should wear black because they are Satan worshippers. In the days that follow, these three boys find themselves gaining the attentions of their peers and teachers, who seem to be watching them. Shawn and his friends begin to play to the audience, saying things like, "We put a curse on the football team." The team loses that week.

Shawn finally has an identity. He need not be anonymous anymore. To live up to their new identity, he and his friends begin reading more about the occult. One day they get some beer, go out into the woods, and concoct a ritual. They talk about making a "blood pact" with each other, and "giving their souls to Satan". Shawn and his friends become increasingly preoccupied with reading, studying and acting out their understandings of satanism. They especially like to focus on sexual freedom and making their own rules. Some teenage girls have started to hang around with them and now the "rituals" usually include sex. Other kids in school begin to keep their distance. Shawn enjoys the feeling that he can scare them just by walking down the hall and glaring. What began as an off-hand comment now has a strong payoff. Shawn is taking it seriously. Satanism has become very real to him and his friends. They make plans to obtain a human skull from a graveyard.

§

Each of these stories relates to activities that can be labeled "satanic." In the first example, the young man uses his readings in *The Satanic Bible*, with their emphasis on smashing people who get in the way, and going against established rules and norms. He fantasizes about revenge against the people in his life who seem to be "in his way" or who place limits upon him. For just a few minutes, in his fantasies, he has some power over the people and situations in his life that seem to control him. In his imagination, he gets to turn the tables. For this young man, it is enough to flirt with readings and imagine himself in a position of power. He may or may not consider himself involved in satanism.

The second story is an example of a common perception of adolescent satanism—a small group of teens who perform ritualistic sacrifice. What has actually happened here, however, seems far less organized and thorough than the popular picture of adolescent satanism. In this example, a few young people who enjoy talking about satanic ideas and practices discover that they can make their peers curious, even afraid. One day they get high together, and two of them intuitively prey on a young woman's wishes to appear mature or independent. She confidently replies, even though she is very uncomfortable with what they are doing. For these teens, killing the cat is not just a prop. They get a certain feeling from doing it...a release of aggressive tension, a connection to each other, a feeling of power. Their satanic activity is short-lived, however. At some point, the drugs become the most interesting part of their get-togethers, and the energy that previously went into creating rituals now goes into obtaining drugs.

The last story shows how some teens may experience tremendous pay-offs and benefits from satanism. They get the attention of teachers, parents and peers with offhand remarks. Shawn, who once was an invisible, ordinary student in a large school, now has a certain notoriety. He becomes part of a small insider's group. The satanic ideology offers Shawn and his friends encouragement to act on their sexual feelings, to seek instant gratification, and to live counter to established authority. By doing so, they gain a certain kind of power over peers and adults who are afraid of them. Some adults see the actions of the youth as based on religious belief, which makes these young people especially powerful. Eventually, some of the adolescents will act out in criminal ways.

## Satan or Power?

It is tempting to assume that what these three very different situations have in common is a focus on Satan. In reality, the figure of Satan becomes a minor character in each of these scenes. The common denominator is the use of satanism to gain power. In one case, that power was limited to fantasies. In the other situations, the teens experienced the power to "hook" the fear of peers and adults, or the power to inflict pain or discomfort on a person or an animal (in one case, involving the *killing* of an animal). When young people get involved in satanism, the worship of an evil supernatural being is of secondary importance. What's most important is the experience of being powerful. In today's society, which seems to multiply the powerlessness of young people and children, the search for opportunities to exert or experience some kind of power in their own lives becomes persuasive.

## Why Power?

Power is a complex concept. It involves the ability to influence one's environment, to determine outcomes, or to exert authority. For example, a baby crying in a concert hall has a lot of power. She can effectively prevent others from hearing and enjoying the performance with her wailing. On the other hand, she lacks the power to rectify the cause of the discomfort—she cannot change her own diaper! In that sense, the baby is powerless.

A police officer summoning a driver to pull over to the side of the road does not have the power to actually *force* the car to move. A person is no match for a car. That makes the driver much more powerful. And yet the police officer possesses a very effective form of power: the ability to arrest the driver. The police officer's power is the authority of law.

Power concerns the ability to determine one's own course of action or that of another person; the ability to make decisions and exert one's wishes. Power is a factor in all kinds of relationships, from parent/child relationships to those among spouses, friends, co-workers, and even nations. Sometimes the power between two people appears to be equal. Two friends, for example, may be equally interdependent with one another in the friendship they have freely chosen. In many relationships, however, power is unequal. The balance of power is tilted in favor of one person. For example, in an employer/employee relationship, the employer possesses more power because they have some say over how the employee spends work time, and over the person's employment in that company.

Generally, children have less power than adults to determine events: parents choose the child's bedtime, clothing, and what they can eat. As children become older, they take, and are given, more responsibility for making decisions and for choices affecting their own lives. This process of increasing responsibility and limited self-determination seems to proceed fairly smoothly for many people, until adolescence.

## Adolescence: Powerfully Powerless

Despite its appearance as a youth-centered culture, contemporary American society shows considerable hostility toward young people. Much of the news about teens focuses on their problems and failings, making them an easy target for scapegoating. "Darn kids...there wouldn't be any crime in this neighborhood if the kids weren't causing trouble." This a familiar kind of statement about youth. City governments pay lip service to the need for constructive alternatives for youth who now "hang out" in streets and shopping areas. But those same governments cut funding in youth centers and youth-related programs.

Teenagers truly live in the world of in-between: no longer children, yet not adults. Many adult expectations come their way— to get jobs, to be more responsible, to look and dress in ways associated with sexual maturity, to make important decisions about their futures. And yet, many of the so-called privileges of adulthood are denied them. They must still depend on parents and adults who can veto their decisions, or they are denied many of the trappings of adulthood which movies, television, and advertising idolize all around them, such as access to alcohol or sexual activity.

The problem of powerlessness becomes compounded by the lack of appropriate "marker events"—rites of passage that mark transitions into greater maturity. In previous times certain items of clothing (for example the wearing of stockings or high heeled shoes for young women) might have been reserved for young people reaching a particular age. But these days, there seem to be few such "markers" related to dress. The ability to play on a competitive sports team, once reserved for high school, now becomes an option for the early elementary student with "pee-wee leagues" and other organized sports opportunities. With the increased secularity and fewer persons who are actively involved as part of a faith community, fewer young people have access to religious "marker events" (bar mitzvah, bat mitzvah, or confirmation) that once served to ritualize transitions of age. The absence of most marker events places teens in a situation of "in-betweenness" over an extended period of time.

The "in-betweenness" of the teen years occurs not only in society, but also as an aspect of adolescent development. We will explore the issues of adolescent development in a later chapter. For now, it is important to note the way in which teens are "mature, yet not mature," in their thinking, their emotional lives, and their spirituality. Young teens may have all the biological prerequisites for sexual activity and strong sexual feelings. But they lack the cognitive ability to make good judgments that fully consider the consequences of sexual involvement. They are ready, and yet, not ready, for sexual intimacy.

Living in such an "in-between" state translates into powerlessness. As images of successful teens and young adults fill their television and movie screens, a young person is bombarded with messages about the benefits of being independent of parental authority. This comes at the very time they are struggling developmentally for some separation from parents. And yet these same young people are powerless to achieve such independence for themselves. After all, they still live at home with parents, have to attend school every day, have limited incomes, and have a curfew.

At a time when adolescents are naturally resistant to authority, authorities set limits on their decision-making power or activities. The powerlessness of adolescent concerns powerlessness over the developmental experiences themselves that shape this time of life. Teens find themselves in a state of terrible self-consciousness that they did not ask for. They do not choose to be so peer-centered. It just happens to them.

In the face of powerlessness, all young people seek out the places in their lives where they do have some power, some say, some ability to influence their environments. Some teens take on jobs to have income that they can spend in whatever way they choose. Others discover that while their parents will not compromise about certain things like curfew, they can choose not to go to church or to style their hair a certain way without getting much resistance from their parents. Finding arenas to exert personal power becomes important for teens. But not all of these arenas are positive.

## Satanic Power

Young people without positive resources may use satanism as a way to acquire some sense of power over people and places in their lives where they feel powerless. For them, satanism in its various forms becomes a power pact, a way of gaining a sense of power in the midst of pervasive powerlessness. Adolescents involved in satanism experience a new and euphoric kind of power that takes on several dimensions: (1) power with peers; (2) power over parents and other adults; (3) power in relation to the fragile self; and (4) power in relation to the supernatural.

## Power Among Peers

Among peers, satanism may elicit responses of curiosity, distaste, admiration, respect and fear. That ability to draw some sort of reaction is powerful among an age group that works so hard to affect boredom. In some cases, the power with the peer group may be coercive or exploitative, as when satanism with its justification of male-dominant sexual activity becomes the vehicle for sexual abuse of a peer. In other instances it takes the form of "power from a distance" as a small group acts in ways that draw fear from peers at school who wonder if this group really can cast spells or curses on them.

Some of the power adolescent satanists experience among their peer group is real—they actually have the ability to stir up fear or to act coercively. Some of their power, however, is perceived power. The teens involved in Satan worship focus on projecting an image to their peers that they can command supernatural forces. In the process, satanic-involved teens may grandiosely perceive themselves to have a level of power beyond reality.

### Power Over Parents and Other Adults

Satanism may be one of the few remaining ways for youth to get a reaction from parents or school authorities. A few hints of satanic beliefs or practices from a teen elicits considerable attention and concern for adults. And in a society tolerant of a variety of behaviors once considered unacceptable, satanism is one of the few ways to be truly "counter-culture" today.

Unfortunately, many young people discover that they can get negative attention much more easily than positive attention from the adults. To be associated with satanic practices adds a certain spark to that negative attention. It seems to really "get under the skin" of adults. Its association with heinous crimes and drug use, besides its direct attack on parental/adult religious beliefs, makes adolescent satanism powerful with adults.

### Power and the Fragile Self

Adolescent satanism has the effect of giving the teen power over the developmental forces from within that are so difficult. Identity problems  are "solved" with participation in a group identified as satanic. The internal struggle against limits imposed by parents or others can be mediated through fantasies, or sometimes the reality, of retaliation against those people—taking power over the ones who exercise power in their lives.

The adolescent problem of developing a personal ethic or value system about sexual behavior disappears in the satanic value of sexual gratification. Issues of low self-esteem are met with satanic language about the self as the center of all. Satanic ideology provides a young person with some sense of power over the personal inner struggles all adolescents face.

## Power and the Supernatural

Most adolescents show a certain fascination with the supernatural. In the upcoming chapter on adolescent development we will explore some of the reasons for that fascination. Sometimes this fascination can be measured in dollars. A quick look at the lines outside the movie theaters will reveal that teens are the major consumers of horror films. Occult (meaning "hidden") refers to things which cannot be known through the senses or through normal means of scientific inquiry. Adolescents are naturally curious about the possibility of gaining access to such hidden things, especially when they know that not everyone has such access.

Because of their developing capacities for abstraction, for distinguishing fantasy from reality, and a need to find reasons and meaning for events that are difficult to explain, teens can become interested in the world of the occult. For young people with no faith tradition, the encounter with the occult may be their first experience with the ideas of a power that is larger than or transcends the self—a power beyond human control.

The notion that a person could gain access to such a power and use it for their own purposes becomes especially appealing to a teenager. After all, so much of life seems out of their control. Teens can feel quite powerless over most of what happens to them. One solution is to have a cosmic-level, secret power that not everyone possesses. And in the complexities and confusions of sorting out the worlds of imagination and reality where magical thinking competes with a more objective ability to assess one's power over events, teens may perceive themselves or others as able to summon supernatural power to influence the world. They see themselves making an alliance with a strong and powerful being or force—the power of evil.

The image portrayed by Anton LaVey certainly feeds into the adolescent fascination with non-material reality. LaVey makes claims of manipulating such unseen forces with spells and ritual magic. And he captivates the imagination of a young audience by dressing the part: pictures of LaVey show a slender, unsmiling man with shaven head, wearing a cape and gazing with a penetrating look that has a supernatural aura.

## Is Power Such a Dirty Word?

The understanding of adolescent satanic involvement as a search for power may suggest that teenagers are power-hungry creatures scavenging the land for ways to acquire more power over the people in their lives. The desire for self-determination, for power to shape and influence one's own world, is a normal and positive desire of human beings. Power does not have to be a negative word. Yet we often associate power with coercion or negativity because of the way people frequently use power *against* one another. The fact that adolescents desire fewer constraints on their decision-making power constitutes a sign of their growth and maturity as persons. The problem comes when those same adolescents find negative ways to attain such power, as is the case with satanism.

## What Does Adolescent Satanism Look Like?

At the conclusion of the first chapter I listed several features of adolescent satanic practice. Most of them run counter to the popular belief that Satan worshipping teens are part of a nation-wide, centrally organized network of satanists who ritualistically and routinely kill animals and humans, use the same religious rituals, and symbols, join established, long-term groups, or are part of the Church of Satan. This is a common image of adolescent satanism. It is an image easily exploited by the news media. But what does adolescent satanism really look like?

Teens who are interested or involved in satanism may be engaging in any number of practices, either on their own or with others. There is no common experience shared by all. For some teens, reading the *Satanic Bible* or occult writings in the privacy of their rooms is the extent of their involvement. For them, it is enough to read with fascination and perhaps fantasize about the occult world. They may not even talk to their peers about their curiosity and interest. Nothing in their behavior changes - they do not appear to be "acting on" their satanic or occult interest. It is one of many interests in their lives.

Other young people involved in satanism join with peers to create ceremonies or rituals. These are sometimes based on readings in books like *The Satanic Rituals*—but more often made up on the spur of the moment. They may do this a few times and then drop it when satanism becomes boring. Or they may discover some excitement in being part of a small group who know secrets and participate in secret rituals that others on the outside can only wonder about with curiosity or, perhaps, fear.

Sixteen year old Jack named himself a "dabbler in satanism". When asked to describe what he meant by this self-designation, Jack replied, "One night while I was using drugs with some kids I just met, some of them decided to do a ritual. I was the lookout, and they sacrificed a dog."

Where did the youths get the idea for this ritual? "They heard that satanic people sacrifice animals," he said. "One guy read about it in the paper and somebody else had a book or something...", Jack said. The incident was Jack's only participation with others in a ritualistic experience, and his involvement was minimal. Yet out of this experience he labels himself as one who dabbles in satanism.

Still other youths may discover that their participation in satanic rituals involves embracing an ideology that appeals to them—one that emphasizes sexual freedom, an anti-authority stance, and the importance of self-gratification. They utilize symbols associated with satanism—the pentagram, goat's head, upside down cross—as an expression of their affiliation with the group that practices this ideology. They may also look for music, literature and films that included explicit depictions of "the demonic" as a way to enhance their experience.

A minority of young people identified with satanism engage in overt criminal activity—vandalism or violence of some kind. It is common in urban areas to see symbols popularly associated with satanism spray-painted on the sides of buildings. The symbols are there not for their religious content but as vandalism. Occasionally one hears of more destructive vandalism, or violence in the form of the killing of animals. Young people also talk about "the sacrifice of babies" or murders as part of satanic ritual. Most of the time these varying degrees of criminal violence are just talk, a way to grab the attention of an audience. Sometimes a crime is labelled satanic "after the fact," as police, reporters, and neighbors seek explanations. But there are some young people who engage in such destructive, criminal activities as grave robbing, sexual abuse and exploitation, bloodletting, harming or killing animals, or serious vandalism which they relate to their satanic ideas.

One of the most destructive aspects of teen satanic practice relates to the way sources such as *The Satanic Bible* condone sexual behavior that victimizes young women. Satanism encourages gender-stereotyped, passive roles for women as objects for male sexual pleasure. The emphasis upon personal physical gratification above all else, and especially above concern for the well-being of another, provide a license for abusive sexual behavior. For adolescents, sorting out the intersection between their strong sexual feelings, confusion about gender roles, and self-esteem problems, the potential for sexual abuse and exploitation is high. If those teens turn to sources such as *The Satanic Bible* for their practices, they can easily find reinforcement for impulsive sexual behavior in the name of sexual freedom.

Pat, a young woman in early adolescence, described feeling unattractive to boys, until she met some older teens with whom she would drink after school. One of these young men suggested that they conduct a "Black Mass" and explained to Pat the central role she would play in the ritual—a role that involved taking off her clothing and stimulating each of the boys sexually.

"We got drunk," she said, "and I thought, 'why not'? They wouldn't want to if they didn't like my body. And, it was supposed to be a really cool thing to do the Black Mass. At that time I felt so bad about myself that I didn't even see how those guys were using me. I was just happy for the attention. I thought they really liked me."

## What About "Ritual Abuse"?

The exploitative and abusive experiences some teens encounter in practicing satanism might lead some people to place teen satanism alongside "ritual abuse." The term may refer to any abusive behavior carried out as part of a ceremony or ritual of some sort (satanic or other). Or it may mean acts of abuse, usually sexual, which are perpetrated in a patterned, "ritualistic" manner.

In recent years, however, the term *ritual abuse* has acquired a more specific meaning, one which should not be confused with the abuse in adolescent satanism. They are not the same.

In some parts of the country during the late 1980s, therapists and other mental health professionals began to hear stories from adult women about forced participation in satanic rituals that occurred in their early childhood. There appeared to be a certain uniformity to these stories. Women who had never spoken to each other and who lived in very different parts of the country identified the same basic experience.

There are some professionals who say they are treating women with a diagnosis of multiple personality disorder "caused by ritual abuse in early childhood." Mental health professionals remain divided on the issue of ritual abuse. Not all practitioners consider multiple personality disorder to be a valid diagnosis. Even though there is considerable agreement among those who do that the disorder has its roots in extremely traumatic experiences in early childhood or infancy, clinicians and theorists remain divided about ritual abuse as a possible origin of the trauma.

It is significant that these reports began to surface around the country shortly after the 1980 publication of a book entitled, *Michelle Remembers*[1], a story written by a woman with assistance from her psychiatrist/husband, recounting her experiences of ritual abuse as a child. Those who believe that such experiences are in fact happening to women all across the nation interpret the proximity of this book's popularity and the influx of stories about ritual abuse during childhood from adult women to mean that women have found "permission" to name what had happened to them—permission to break the social norm against talking about abuse.

Others are troubled by the lack of physical evidence to substantiate the stories of ritual abuse, which often include stories about murder or fetal sacrifice. The remains have not been found. The bodies have not been found. The physical evidence does not appear to bear out these stories. And yet it is clear that something extremely traumatic and abusive has occurred for the women who tell these stories. Those who question the lack of evidence tend to view differently the connection between popularity of the book *Michelle Remembers* and the telling of ritual abuse stories. This group sees the image of ritual abuse as a vehicle for women to put language to something so traumatic that it has been unspeakable, instead of understanding it as evidence that large numbers of women have experienced ritual abuse at the hands of satanists. "Ritual abuse" provides a metaphor, a way of naming a woman's experience of incredible chaos, pain and evil.

Whatever one believes about the validity of satanic ritual abuse as the cause of mental illness or dysfunction for adult women, it is important to remember two concerns. First, historically it often has been difficult for women to get persons to take seriously their experiences of abuse or oppression. Such experiences have frequently been discounted by health care professionals, clergy, and family members of the women. Regardless of the source of their trauma and abuse, women who find the courage to begin talking about abuse need support and help.

Second, it is important to distinguish the phenomenon of ritual abuse from adolescent satanic practices. While adolescents engaging in satanism do sometimes participate in harmful, abusive ritualistic behaviors, their situation bears little resemblance to the picture suggested in adult stories of ritual abuse. That picture portrays children and young people lured into a secret sect against their will by secretly satanic adults who force them to participate in abusive ritualistic experiences. It suggests a picture of extreme organization and uniformity around the nation, an organization of secret satanic cult groups. While adolescent satanic practices may involve ritual, and may be quite abusive, especially, to young women, they remain a far cry from the practices of childhood ritual abuse.

## How Significant Is Adolescent Satanism?

The subject of adolescent satanism seems to call forth extreme responses. Some people choose to discount adolescent satanism all together, suggesting that it is only as significant as the news media makes it. Some people have called satanism "the Red Scare of the 1990s," seeing in it similarities to McCarthyism. Because of a reactionary tendency to label every crime or murder or every dead animal found in a park as evidence of the satanic, many people decide to disregard the whole phenomenon as invalid. Others consider satanism insignificant because they do not believe the character of Satan exists. Seeing Satan as mythical, or "unreal" means understanding adolescent satanism as insignificant or "unreal".

Still other people conclude that adolescent satanism must be taken seriously as a religious phenomenon - as the vehicle through which an evil being, Satan, exerts power in modern times. Those on this end of the response continuum tend to see adolescents engaged in satanic activity as literally possessed by the Devil. How can we make sense of adolescent satanism in the face of these extreme perspectives? What is its significance?

## When Things Are Not What They Appear To Be

Adolescent satanism is a significant phenomenon and should not be discounted. It is not, however, primarily a "religious" experience for its participants.

What constitutes a religious phenomenon? A minimal definition of religion is that it provides its believers with a coherent world view that offers a sense of how the universe is ordered, a way to understand life and "make meaning" out of life experiences. To view adolescent satanism as a religious experience is to understand the involvement of teens in practices associated with satanism as being about a world view, a way of understanding life and the ordering of reality. It suggests that they have a "satanic theology."

## The Theology of Religious Satanists

Persons who belong to the Church of Satan might be described as "religious satanists" in that they participate in a group which offers a particular world view. There exists a "theology" of sorts, a way of understanding reality, some commonly held beliefs and related practices. As we saw in an earlier chapter, the world view of the Church of Satan sees human existence in terms of self-gratification as the ultimate source of meaning. The Church of Satan maintains a perspective that the world is directed by forces of nature, identified with the figure of Satan, that can be "tapped into" by persons for their own purposes. Rather than claiming "disbelief" in God, the Church of Satan views God as a human construct, created by people out of weakness. Satan is described as "a hidden force in nature, responsible for the workings of early affairs". Persons for whom satanism is a religion, find a world view that answers such basic questions as, "What is the relationship between human beings and other creatures," and "Who's in charge?" It provides a lens through which to see reality and assign meaning to life experiences.

## Adolescent Satanists and the Absence of a "Theology"

In contrast, adolescent satanism does not concern a particular way of understanding reality. It is marked by what the young person does *not* believe rather than expressing a particular system of belief or a tradition. Jim, a teen in a chemical dependency treatment aftercare program, was having a great deal of difficulty at home after completing treatment. Although he attended a structured aftercare program everyday and followed most of its requirements, his behavior suggested that something was wrong. He isolated himself from his peers, and appeared preoccupied. He was having major arguments at home again because his parents enforced the curfews that were part of the contract Jim made before leaving treatment to help him in his recovery.

Finally, one of his peers in the aftercare group confronted him with the knowledge that Jim was using drugs again. Jim returned to treatment briefly. But he continued to keep to himself. And when it came time for Jim to share with his peers his understanding of a Higher Power and of the 2nd and 3rd Steps of A.A., he completely withdrew from the group and refused to talk.

"I don't believe in God," Jim shouted.

His counselors assured him that he need not profess belief in *God* to use the A.A. program for recovery. Instead, he needed to identify someone or something as a Higher Power that could help him.

"Satan is my Higher Power," Jim finally said.

Jim acknowledged his involvement in satanism, and that drug use was connected to it.

"I don't believe in God," he repeated.

But when asked to describe what he *did* believe in, and to describe his understanding of Satan, Jim spoke only in terms of that which he rejected.

"The Bible talks about how God is so great and does so many good things," he said. "Well, God never did anything good for me, so I don't believe in God. I don't believe in the Bible either."

For Jim and other adolescents, satanism offers a way to stand in opposition to traditional religious beliefs and practices, rather than providing a particular world view that young people can embrace. They can articulate clearly what they do *not* believe, but have trouble stating what they mean when they say that Satan is their Higher Power or that they worship Satan.

## A Case of Mistaken Identity

In a quiet auditorium, a policeman speaks to an audience giving him rapt attention. He shows slides of graffiti or vandalism which is the work of satanists and offers statistics about how many crimes are linked to satanic activity. At the close of the meeting a pastor is invited to pray for "our young people whose souls are at stake". The prayer includes concerns about teenagers who are falling prey to demonic powers everywhere—in rock music, in the break-up of the family, everywhere Satan is lurking. The prayer ends with requests to God that young people might increase their faith and thereby be protected from involvement in satanism.

The people attending the meeting listened in the hope that the police department's cult crimes expert could help them quiet their fears. The problem is that they, like the policeman and the pastor at the meeting, are misunderstanding the issue. Because adolescent satanism has the appearance, feel and language of a religious issue, these people all assume that adolescent satanism is a religious phenomenon. But adolescent satanism is not about young people falling prey to demonic powers. It is about young people acting out and then finding counter-cultural religious beliefs to provide a structure and rationale for their actions.

## Neither Religion Nor Faith

Adolescent satanism is not about religion. Nor is it about faith. The distinction between religion and faith may be insignificant for some people. But such a distinction helps in understanding the nature of adolescent satanism. Religion concerns a world view, a way of understanding reality. It is made up of traditions and some commonly held precepts or "beliefs" expressing that world view. It employs ritual as a means of participating in that part of reality which stands outside of ordinary experience. Faith is a quality of trust and loyalty to "a transcendent center of value and power." [2] Faith is a way of being and living in the world, based on trust and fidelity to a "Higher Power", something that transcends the self. It has less to do with agreement with a set of doctrines than with the quality of action, relationship, and identity. Faith concerns the direction of a person's life energies and values, and how those are lived out.

Adolescent satanism is not about faith. Despite its appearances of being focused on a relationship with a transcendent being, Satan, which provides a center point for how one lives, adolescent satanism rarely involves a "relationship" with Satan. Instead, teens utilize the figure of Satan as a way to establish their behaviors and attitudes over and against traditional religious beliefs. They do not "set their heart." [3] on Satan in a relationship of trust and loyalty. They may see themselves as establishing an alliance with Satan or evil or the demonic, but this alliance differs substantially from faith.

What do teens mean when they say they worship Satan? They mean that they are involved in some behaviors and practices which they associate with satanism, and that they reject more commonly held religious perspectives of the adults in their lives. The difficulty is that adolescent satanism can look a lot like religion—it uses symbols and rituals, it deals with beings and objects identified in religions such as Christianity, Judaism, and Islam (Satan, demons, God); it employs language about good and evil powers; and it concerns the supernatural, an area traditionally associated with religious belief. And yet, despite all these religious trappings, adolescent satanists are not primarily engaged in a religious activity. Rather, the appearance of satanism as a religious phenomenon masks its actual identity as a phenomenon of adolescent development combined with the current social conditions of American culture.

## If Not Religion, Then What Is It ?

Adolescent satanism may best be understood as a phenomenon of adolescent developmental dynamics and group dynamics, with religious/ritualistic overtones. In its most developed expressions it predominantly appears among chemical-using, disenfranchised, emotionally-troubled teens. It is an outward expression of the young person's difficulty negotiating developmental transitions and family issues. Adolescent satanism also emerges out of a particular societal condition in which satanic practices are among the few remaining means by which young people can simultaneously express discontent and claim power.

Adolescent satanism fundamentally concerns power. It is a power pact, an agreement unwittingly made between the young person, parents or other adults, the peer group, and society. Adolescent satanism provides a way for young people who experience a great deal of powerlessness in their lives to claim some power.

### Relating Adolescent Development to Satanism

Adolescent satanism is a developmental phenomenon. That does not mean that all teens go through a period of satanic activity as part of their development! Rather, the nature of what young people work through in the developmental journey makes adolescence a time when satanism becomes especially attractive to some teens.

What are the implications of viewing satanism as an adolescent development issue? One implication is that different options for responding to satanism will emerge. A second implication concerns who is affected by teen satanism. If satanism relates to adolescent developmental issues, then a variety of young people from diverse circumstances may be attracted to it. This leads to a third implication, prevention of the dangers that can result when teens practice satanism. Prevention requires an understanding of the nature of adolescent development.

Five key aspects of adolescent development related to satanic activity are:

- the peer-centered culture of adolescence
- sexuality
- authority issues
- the establishment and integration of the adolescent's self-concept (identity issues)
- the need for an "updated" world view/faith perspective appropriate to adolescence

These five issues will be explored in the next chapter.

# Chapter 3

## ADOLESCENT DEVELOPMENT

*"It seemed like he just woke up one day and was different. One day he was my little boy, my son...the next day he was this rude, obnoxious thing living in my house like it was his private hotel—and like I was the maid!"*

—Mother of a fourteen-year-old boy

*"Yeah, I think about it a lot. Like, when am I gonna get to go on weekend trips with my boyfriend? I mean, I'm gonna be in high school soon. My parents are really changing. They used to trust me. Now they always seem to want to know where I'm going and who I'm with and will there be alcohol there. They treat me like I'm a little kid."*

—Twelve-year-old girl

*"My dad wants to control everything about me. He can try. He even tries to make me believe what he does about God. I have my own thoughts. I might even have my own god...there's a lot he doesn't know about me."*

—Fifteen-year-old

What happens to human beings when they become teenagers? Is adolescence a mutation? Can this behavior possibly be normal? Why do teens act the way they do?

It's not surprising that questions like these come up in any conversation about teenagers. After all, many adults who are parents share the experience of the mother I have quoted, in which their "little boy" or "little girl" seems to disappear overnight, is replaced by an alien of some kind who eats unusual food, speaks a foreign language, has strange looking companions, and avoids being seen with the family at all costs. For other parents, the experience of a son's or daughter's move into adolescence may be more gradual and less traumatic.

There are many places to get stuck on the journey of adolescent development, and many opportunities for problems. But there exists just as many opportunities for positive growth and creative problem-solving. Here are the top ten items one group of parents enjoys about their teenagers:

1. It's fun to watch them becoming more of their own person.

2. We can have more of a relationship—can really talk about important things and enjoy doing some things together in a more mutual way.

3. They have so many more opportunities than we did at their age, and it's very exciting to watch the possibilities unfold for them.

4. Teenagers are so playful and spontaneous.

5. It's encouraging to see their growing sense of responsibility.

6. Youthful idealism makes me feel hopeful about the world.

7. Teens are full of surprises—we never get bored.

8. Their energy can be contagious.

9. It's very moving to see what caring persons they are becoming.

10. The more independent they are, the more independence we have as parents. It's really nice for us to have these people who are part of the family but who do more and more for themselves.

The teen years do not have to be crisis-filled. They are not automatically disastrous for the young person or the family. There are many, many bright spots to this life period we call adolescence. But when a young person becomes a teenager, it changes the entire family.

It can seem to young people as if their parents are the ones doing the changing, not themselves. The twelve-year-old girl cited finds herself wondering what has come over her parents. To her they seem victims of a new paranoia, always worried about what *might* happen to her. And lately they've become so nosey! Always wanting to know her business, always asking to be introduced to her friends...and suddenly they seem so, well, so *old*.

For some teens, it feels as if parents have launched an active campaign to keep them from growing up. At other times, it may feel as if parents are practically throwing them out the door with jet propulsion devices attached to their backs!

The question of what is happening in adolescence, both for the individual teen and the family, is complicated by the fact that there is no "correct" way that people experience adolescence. A person's experience is determined by factors as diverse as individual temperament, economic situation, cultural community, geographical location, family coping style, and community support networks. Despite these individual variations, we can point to some common features in the adolescent developmental process. As we will see in the following chapters, many of these developmental aspects can help explain why adolescence is a time ripe for attraction to satanism.

### Beginning With Baby

Once upon a time every person who is now a teenager was a baby. Some were cute and cuddly, others were crying and colicky. Some people believe that of any two life stages, infancy and adolescence share the most in common, in terms of what is required for the person to grow and develop. There also seems to be a relationship between difficulties experienced on the developmental journey by the infant, and those experienced by the adolescent.

From the perspective of development, the most amazing thing about babies is how so much is compressed in a short period of time. From the beginning of life to the ripe old age of three, babies cram an awful lot of developmental change into their days. It happens fast. In only hours, a baby moves from the warmth and security of the womb to the outside world. Even the first few hours of a baby's life are a process of adapting to changes. The baby must adjust from being physically attached to the mother, to being physically separate but emotionally fused. At this time of the baby's life there exists a kind of "symbiotic union" in which the baby experiences itself and the mother as one. When the baby cries, milk arrives or comforting arms pick the baby up. To the baby, the mother is an extension of the self. It is common today to speak of the "bonding" between babies and their parents. Bonding refers to the remarkable circle in which both baby and parents experience deep emotional connection. As the parent, through smiles and caring attention, reflects back to the baby that she/he is loved and valued, the baby gradually gains a sense of the self as lovable and valuable. But at first, there is no awareness that the parent is an "other", separate from the self. The baby is the center of the universe.

Then one day, the baby cries and nothing happens. No bottle or breast is presented. No arms reach out. The baby begins to realize that this amazing being who brings food and comfort is in fact a separate creature. As motor skills develop and babies explore their own body boundaries, they become more aware of themselves as separate creatures. "These toes way down there are mine!" babies discover as they grab for their toes and play with their feet. The main experience of the baby between ages two months to six months is that of being a body. As psychiatrist Daniel Stern has discovered in his research on infant development, babies use their bodies to elicit expressions and behaviors from their caretakers.

Have you ever noticed the way a parent gazes into a baby's eyes and displays facial expressions that would look silly to an adult? Babies have their own repertoire of behaviors designed to elicit these expressions of care. According to Stern, babies do not act as sponges, passively receiving what their parents offer toward building a relationship. Instead they are immediately "partner[s] in shaping [their] first and foremost relationships."[1]

As crawling gives way to toddling, babies seem to delight in this experience of the awareness of separation. "Look at me! I can go anywhere," they seem to say. And they delight in practicing their newfound abilities to literally stand on their own two feet and be a separate self. But the ability to stand apart depends very much upon a sense of secure attachment. Babies who toddle away from their parents engage in frequent "checking back" behaviors, as if to say, "Are you still watching me? How far away can I go and still be safely connected?" Checking back provides a kind of emotional refueling that allows the baby to continue practicing separation.

And then the crisis comes. At some point in this marvelous experimentation with mobility and separation, it dawns on the baby that "if I can go away from them, then they can go away from me too." Parents of young children often remark that just when they begin to feel a little freedom with their baby, suddenly, that child becomes clingy again, reacts with fear or shyness toward strangers, and seems afraid of being alone. The child reacts to the fear of separation with increased demands for attachment.

How does this separation crisis get resolved? Around age three, children consolidate an ability that they have been developing for a while—the ability to conjure up an image of the parent that is associated with trust and safety. This internal image is available to the child when the child feels distressed about the absence of the parent. The child's ability to draw on the internalized comforting image of the parent in order to cope with separation is called "object constancy." The word "object" is unfortunate because it sounds cold and sterile, but it refers to the one who is the object of the baby's desires for attachment, safety and love. To develop such constancy, children use things associated with the safe presence of the parent, such as blankets, toys, or pacifiers. This helps them cope when the parent is not there. These traditional objects are important for the child to tolerate separation in the face of the anxiety it creates.

This process, from the initial emotional "oneness" with the parent, toward the establishment of a separate sense of self, is a kind of "psychological birth." It is known as the separation-individuation process of development. [2] It is a description of the series of changes infants go through as they grow into their own unique individuated sense of self. Obviously, our development does not end at age three. We continue to renegotiate relationships with others throughout our lives, looking for optimal levels of connection and separation. Our entire lives as human beings are marked by these changes. Our growth and development depend on them. That is to say, development is a relational process. It happens in the experience of relationship with others, particularly those significant others called parents. Adolescence marks a time of major re-negotiation in relationships, and an active revisiting of the developmental issues of infancy. In a strange way, infancy is the backdrop for the teen years.

### All Grown Up . . . Well, Sort of

Usually the term adolescence refers to the years between age eleven to age eighteen. These are years of intense physical, emotional, spiritual, and social maturation. The young person lets go of many childhood dependencies, creates new and different kinds of attachments, and moves into a state of greater personal autonomy in the approach toward adulthood. Adolescence as a life-stage, and teens themselves, get a lot of "bad press". It is a time often fraught with upheaval, confusion and difficulty.

What makes this time so difficult for the young person, psychologically, is essentially, the same thing that made the separation process difficult for the infant. In exchange for a greater degree of psychological separation, more independence and autonomy, the young person must give up the more familiar and certain security of childhood dependency. It is not always an easy exchange. This developmental shift can be thought of as a grief experience, a loss of sorts, as the young person says goodbye to

childhood.³   Much of the moodiness associated with young
adolescence relates to this grief.  It is not uncommon for a young
person to want permission to go out with friends in the evening
independent of parental supervision, only to turn around and resist
throwing out a favorite childhood toy.  For the toddler who checks
back to make sure parents are still watching, it is the connection
with the parents that allows the separation to occur.  Similarly, the
young adolescent will touch base with the familiar, more dependent style of relating to the family while at the same time making
overtures toward greater independence.  This can be very difficult
for parents!  The same hug that was just a few hours ago sought
out by the young person is now an unwelcome intrusion on
budding independence.  In a sense, teens *are* all grown up, ready
to go out and conquer the world.  And yet in many ways they still
lack the thinking ability and social experience to use good
judgement consistently, make good decisions, or solve complex
problems.  All grown up?  Well, sort of.

### Portrait of a Teenager

Recently I asked a group of parents to draw a composite picture
of a "typical" teen.  Some of the features of their drawing provide
a helpful way to think about the distinguishing developmental
features of adolescence.  The picture showed a person wearing
jeans with a recognizable brand insignia on the pocket; long hair
drawn to look "wild"; ears pierced in several places, with one long
dangling earring that looked like a religious symbol; headphones
apparently playing loud music; and a slight case of facial acne.  One
hand held a can of Coca Cola.  The other held a bag of potato chips,
labeled "Junk Food to the Max".  There was a telephone in the
picture, and in the distance several friends also had telephones.
Slung around the teenager's shoulder was a backpack, with sports

equipment and brand name athletic shoes spilling out. Barely visible in this backpack was a can that looked as if it might be a beer can. But the parents who drew the picture said they "could not be sure." They also "could not tell for sure" if the little envelope barely sticking out of the wallet was a condom. A sign reading "Keep, out, especially kid brothers" was plastered across the door of the room where the young person stood. One wall showed a poster of a rock star. Another wall had a poster of a lone adventurer climbing up a steep cliff, and the caption, "Go for it!"

The drawing illustrates some of the features of adolescent development. It is a time of conformity and peer centeredness. And yet it is a time of establishing a unique sense of self. Adolescence is a time of heightened sexual awareness, sexual experimentation, and value development. During adolescence, struggling with authority—especially parental authority—is part of the process of separation from parents. So is the desire for greater privacy. Young people use clothing, hairstyle, music, and friends as a way to experiment with different roles and try on different identities. They have heroes and heroines, and fantasies of what they themselves can become. And it is, of course, a time of important physical, emotional and mental change.

## From Concrete to Abstract

Young children think concretely. When asked to describe "home" children six to ten years of age will talk about a particular place they live. Home means that place. The move toward abstract thinking happens over several years. But at some point, when asked to describe "home," a young person will say: "Home is the place where I feel I belong. It's where we live as a family."

With increasing capacity for abstract thinking comes the ability to move beyond literal understandings of symbols to a more abstract understanding. Instead of a direct association (a literal correspondence of the symbol with what it represents), abstract thinking abilities allow symbols to function metaphorically. A symbol is a metaphor—it stands for, or represents, something beyond itself. For example, with the ability to think abstractly, a wedding ring may stand for one's commitment to the spouse, or may represent something else. But the ring itself does not equate with commitment. The ability to abstract, and the use of symbols to represent meanings beyond the object itself, is a critical part of the social, psychological, and religious development of teens. Most teens, especially younger youth, waiver back and forth between concrete thinking and the beginnings of abstract thought. The "full-blown" capacity for abstract thinking does not develop until late adolescence.

Abstract thought also opens up the world of the "double entendre" to teens, the realization that a word or phrase can have multiple meanings. One of those meanings might be sexual or illicit, adding to the excitement. Any junior high teacher can recount multiple examples of the phrase used in innocence that sets the whole class into hysterics. *"I'm passing out this paper..." "Hey, John, she's passing out, catch her quick!" "Passing out? What, did ya have too much to drink last night?"* While this new language capacity is the headache of many an adult who lives or works with teens, such abilities set the stage for further development of a new sense of self, one that includes the integration of sexual identity.

The beginning of abstract thinking is for the adolescent what early motor skills are for the infant: a world expanding tool that allows movement beyond the familiar. Just as the ability to crawl and then to walk marked the infant's journey toward separation from the mother and eventual individuation, abstract thought marks the separation experience of teens. It allows teens to consider ideas that may be quite different from those voiced in the family, and to establish some points of ideological or even moral differentiation between themselves and the family. For the first time teens are able to reflect on their family's values—and to differentiate themselves.

## Idealistic Thinking

*"My parents say wearing seat belts should be each person's private choice—but I think it should be a law, because if we have a crash, and somebody isn't wearing a seat belt, their private choice affects other people. Ya know, that makes my parents seem pretty selfish, only thinking about whether or not they feel like wearing their seat belt. What if they got killed not wearing theirs and somebody had to go to jail?"*

*"If I want to smoke, that's my decision. They're my lungs, and if I want to ruin them, then it's my problem. That's what you always say to me when I tell you to wear your seat belt—Why should you worry about it if it doesn't hurt you? It's not like I'm smoking in the house. You don't even have to breathe it—so get off my back."*

Teens can be extremely idealistic in their thinking. An appropriate subtitle for the life stage of adolescence is "the anti-hypocrisy crusader years." Abstract thinking capabilities contribute to the way teens are acutely aware of the contradictions in saying and doing, especially by their parents. It allows them to differentiate themselves from others and claim some values as their own. The developing moral idealism of youth fuels their energy for important causes and social change movements. They can play the role of "the nation's conscience" as was the case during the Vietnam War. But to find oneself the target of such idealism can be very uncomfortable!

## New Ways of Thinking

One aspect of adolescent identity formation is the need to establish what is unique about the self. What makes me special? How am I different from everyone else? These questions appear in the inner experience of young adolescents because of a newly acquired ability to reflect on the self. Adolescence marks the beginning of what is called "formal operational thinking." This means that adolescents can view themselves as others might be viewing them. They can construct in their minds how others see them—e.g., "I must look really stupid."

Here is the origin of the terrible self-consciousness of teenagers. They become incredibly concerned about what others are thinking about them. Teens, especially in early adolescence, are certain that everyone else is thinking just like they are—that is, about them! The opinions and expectations of others, especially peers, become critical in how teens experience themselves. So adolescence becomes a time of conformity. Young teens, thinking about themselves objectively (from the perspective of others) judge themselves and then project that picture onto an "imaginary audience" that goes with them everywhere and observes their every move. Such self-preoccupation, sometimes called "normal narcissism," is a necessary part of their development, similar to the infant's experience of the self as the center of the universe.

Adolescents create an ongoing and changing internal story about who they are. This story is drawn from their fantasies, their "ideal self" and incorporation of their heroines and heroes into their own story. As part of shaping a world view and identity, everything—school, friends, parents, the self—is measured against this inner story. Healthy development requires that adolescents learn how to deal with the parts of who they are that do not conform to their construction of an "ideal self." Integrating the "shadow side" of the concept of one's self, developing the capacity for self-forgiveness and for forgiving others, is a lifelong process that begins to take on more important meaning in adolescence.

## The Peer-Centered Culture of Teens

The capacity for formal operational thinking also means that teens develop new abilities to put themselves in the position of another, to "wear another person's shoes," and therefore to show empathy. This creates a deepened capacity for relationships with others. Indeed peer relationships become central in the lives of teens, and a sense of belonging among peers becomes critical. During the teen years, self-esteem and acceptance by one's peer group are closely related.

Attachments to others, for teens attachment to others outside the family, especially peers, helps the teen let go of old ways of relating to family. Young people prefer to spend more time with friends than family. Sometimes they even act embarrassed to be seen with the family. One young man told me that he doesn't mind going shopping with his mom as long as he doesn't have to walk with her in the mall—someone might see them!

The telephone is a primary symbol of adolescence in America. A friend of mine jokes that "adolescence is the time when parents have to ask teenagers for permission to use the telephone for a few minutes!" What creates in teens such an intense need to talk to someone outside of the family? Dr. David Elkind, an expert on adolescent development and health, says that the main reason teenagers talk on the telephone so much is to give the busy signal to other teenagers! He is referring, of course, to that imaginary audience that the young person has—an imaginary audience of peers who will think that the young person has a lot of friends if the phones stays busy!

There is another explanation to the phenomenon of teen "telephone-itis." The developmental journey of the adolescent involves expanding the boundaries—this time, beyond the family unit as the primary sphere of relationship, to a wider world of self-chosen friends. In our culture, the telephone is part of the process of expanding the boundaries of associations and attachments. Like infancy, adolescence is a time of practicing separateness and seeking new attachments. And, as was true for the infant, the successful process of standing on one's own depends on two key features: (1) a trust in the relationships with family (the sense of being loved and valued) that can serve as home base for venturing out on one's own; and (2) encounters with others that allow for the formation of new attachments, promoting a stronger sense of identity and permitting the renegotiation of the former relationships.

### Forming An Identity and Belonging to a Peer Group

Adolescence is a time of discovering and forming personal identity. That means it is a time of experimenting, of trying on different roles, and testing out different ways of being. In this process, teenagers struggle to bring together how others see and respond to them with how they experience themselves. The girl who decides to go to school with spiked hair is running a grand experiment. By the end of the day she learns that her parents think she looks ridiculous. Teachers act like they don't notice...but it seemed like she got in trouble today for things they usually don't pay attention to. Seventh grade girls think she looks "radical"— they like it and want to sit with her at lunch. Seventh grade boys look mystified but intrigued, if not intimidated. Maybe the next day she will try something different. But already today she has gained some important information in shaping her understanding of self.

She has also tested the boundary between how "different" she can be, and still be acceptable to her peers and to certain adults.

## Personal Authority and Identity

For the teenager it can be difficult to merge conflicting perspectives into a unified sense of self. And because teens still rely on external sources as authorities, even for their sense of self, they tend to "compartmentalize," acting one way around friends and another around adults. "My mom thinks I'm lazy. My teacher thinks I'm smart. My friends think I'm cool because I can joke around and still get OK grades. Who am I?" If external sources like other people are still the main source of authority, then identity is likely to depend on who is around. Toward middle and later adolescence teens can validate from within the rationale for what they do, think, or are.

Before teens develop this ability, such decisions depend on personal loyalties or sanctioning by the peer group. A young person may give implicit approval to a particular adult or peer based on some quality in the relationship that encourages loyalty ("I like Mr. Davis—he talks about football in class." Or, "Steve is cool—we like the same music."), or other characteristics that foster loyalty such as racial or ethnic group identification. But the primary authority for what the young person knows or holds true is the peer group ("Everybody thinks Dave is a geek." Or, "Ms. Johnson is a fun teacher—everybody likes her.")

## Rebellion and Identity

Another angle to the authority issue is: "Who gets to say what I do or don't do?" Adolescence provides a young person with mental capacities for rational thinking that cause them to question authority. As part of the process of separation and consolidating their own sense of identity, teens demand reasons. "Because I said so" no longer functions as a valid reason.

All across America, parents and teens are engaging in some variation of the following dialogue:

> Parent: "Do you know what time it is?"
> Teen: "Yeah. So I'm a little late. What's the big deal?"
> Parent: "The big deal is that we have a rule in this house that you have to be home by midnight."
> Teen: "That's a dumb rule. Nobody else has to be home by midnight."
> Parent: "What other people do is their problem. The rule here is midnight. Dumb or not, that's the rule. And as long as you're living in my house, you'll live by my rules."
> Teen: "Then it's a good thing I don't have to live here much longer."

Part of the separation experience entails testing and rebelling against authority, including parental authority. In some teens this takes relatively mild forms such as testing curfew boundaries or voicing "anti-establishment" sentiments designed to push parental buttons. For other teens, though, the struggle against authority means one or more high-risk behaviors—legal violations, sexual acting out, unsafe driving, or drug use.

A young person who questions authority is on a quest toward the more principled reasoning that only develops fully during adulthood. As a step toward that adult state, adolescents move from acceptance of authority based on someone's position ("I'm the mom—what I say goes") to adding their own rational thought which is strongly influenced by relationships, to the granting of authority ("My coach says I can't smoke if I want to play ball. I really like my coach. He can relate to what kids go through and isn't so old-fashioned. And it's true that when I smoke, it affects my quickness on the field."). At issue is who gets to have control. If teens cannot have complete control over what they must do, they at least want to give control to legitimate authorities of their own choosing.

## Sexuality and Identity

How young people feel about their bodies reflects how they feel about themselves. Adolescence is a time of major physical change and development. Early adolescence is marked by the beginning of puberty, as hormones signal changes in the body. Boys experience the appearance of facial and pubic hair, deepening of the voice, enlargement of sexual organs, and ejaculation. Girls experience the growth of pubic hair, breast development and the onset of menstruation. Both experience intensified attractions.

With these changes and heightened sexual awareness comes the need to renegotiate relationships, both within and outside of the family. Establishing body boundaries may occur in the form of increased desire for privacy. Adolescence is also a time of sexual experimentation, acting on attractions within relationships or through self-stimulation. Sexual attraction brings a new factor, and intensity, into peer relationships. It also raises the stakes, because of the possibility of a new kind of rejection. Self-esteem related to the body image can be quite fragile.

Adolescents must negotiate how sexual feelings and behaviors fit with emerging personal values and morality. This task becomes much more difficult for youth whose environment is either "value-rigid" or so-called "value-free."

Value-rigid environments are atmospheres in which one's sense of being a "good person" depends on adherence to the right rules: *Sex is wrong. Our religion is the one right way to think and believe. If you steal you are bad.* What is often termed a value-free environment offers no guidelines for shaping values or making moral decisions: *Do what you want to do. If it feels good, do it. Be true to yourself above all else.* One of the ways young people can get value ownership in a rigid atmosphere is through rebellion and overthrow of the "absolutes" they have been given. In a value-free atmosphere, young people may be left with a trial-and-error approach, choosing their own moral standards through a process of ruling out what feels bad. Determining some guidelines for sexual expression is part of the teen's task of integrating sexuality into their new identity.

"It seems like these kids spend most of their time falling in love and breaking up!" remarked a parent reflecting on adolescent sexuality and relationships. There is some truth to this remark. Along with providing a significant attachment that facilitates separation from the family and sexual expression, romantic relationships offer teens a way to encounter themselves. Teenagers fall in love to discover themselves. They hunger for what the other person sees in them, and to have this person's views reflected back. "I can't believe that she thinks I'm such a hunk—but I sure like it!" There *is* a kind of healthy narcissism to adolescence, a self-preoccupation that helps form an identity.

I am not suggesting that there is no personal attachment to the loved one. But commitments made by teenagers in relationships have at least as much to do with loving/committing to the self as they are a commitment to the other person. Because the adolescent is a "self in transition," many relationships are also transitional.

## It Happens to Families Too

So far we have been looking at adolescent development from the perspective of the individual's passage from childhood to young adulthood. Adolescence is also a developmental process experienced by families. Both the adolescent and the family system go through a change. Some persons and families weather these changes without much difficulty. But even in these families, where the difficulties from change remains fairly low, there is still some stress as the family system adapts to a new reality. In other families, the changes of adolescence brings about crisis.

Not all of the stress relates to the teenager. Adolescence can be a tough time for families because of what happens to parents. Social science researchers half-jokingly refer to the period of time when parents have teens at home as the parents' "middle-essence".[4] Parents often reach career plateaus at this time in their lives. Parents who were homemakers experience role loss as their children become less dependent upon them. Many parents find themselves asking similar questions to the ones posed by their teenagers, questions about the values they hold, the choice they have made. "Is this it? Is this all there is?" Questions like these haunt many middle-aged adults. The presence of one or more critical teenagers merely exacerbates the discomfort.

Frequently, parents see their youthful selves in their teenagers. Teens become a living reminder of missed opportunities or mistakes made along the way. An adolescent frequently bears a striking resemblance to the way a spouse looked in the "Golden Days" of the relationship. If the relationship is troubled or has ended in a divorce such an unconscious daily reminder may be difficult. If parents are also making difficult decisions concerning the care of their own aging parents, the home may feel more like a pressure cooker than a family residence.

## Making Connections:
## The Developmental Process and Teen Satanism

So far we have walked through the process by which adolescents develop toward adulthood. It is a time of amazing parallels to infancy. If a baby lacks the secure attachments that allow her/him to venture out and explore the world, growth will be affected. When the same person becomes an adolescent, and must go through a similar emotional process of venturing out into the world, the old unresolved issues of the infant experience will probably come up again. The baby who had difficulty resolving the "separation crisis" of infancy will likely experience a heightened sense of crisis about the separations necessary in adolescence.

Just as the baby celebrates her or his newfound freedom by toddling around beyond the reach of the parent, the adolescent celebrates new levels of independence and an expanded world: the ability to drive a car, to be out with friends without parental supervision, even the opportunity to choose one's own friends. All these are aspects of the teen's growth and maturation that recall in an amplified form the baby's first moves out into the world. But in the same way that it was important for that baby to "check back" (making certain that the parent was not too far away), teens who venture out into the wider world need the security of a "home base", a reliable environment where that young person can be affirmed and cared for. Even though adolescents often manifest a stormy relationship with their families and resist the connection to their home, if such an environment is lacking or absent, the process of forming their own identity is much more difficult to accomplish.

While the adolescent developmental experience should not be understood as a one-to-one correspondence with the infant separation process, the emotional issues to be worked through are quite similar. There seems to be a relationship between how a person experiences the first years of life and how they experience adolescence. The experiences of secure attachments to parents and care providers in infancy set up the possibility for a young person to cope well with the various changes in attachments and other adolescent problems.

It is easy for parents to blame themselves. "If only I had been at home more." "She is having these problems because we didn't hold her enough." Are parents at fault when teens encounter problems? The experiences of infancy and early childhood do provide the foundations for healthy development. But humans are amazingly resilient creatures. We are capable of "bouncing back" from difficulties. Parents are not perfect. They are people who try to offer their children the best possible opportunities to grow. Mistakes happen along the way. But even if parents *could* be perfect, their task would remain difficult. Children come with their own personalities, abilities, and temperament. A young person's ability to cope with the challenges of adolescence involves much more than their early childhood experiences. It includes their unique abilities, their "personal resources." And it is affected by external features like the presence of caring teachers, the family's economic situation, or their town's commitment to supporting teens.

We have also looked at some dimensions of adolescent development for the family, and some of the places where problems are likely to occur. Adolescence is not only an individual's journey. It takes place within a particular family and cultural environment that shapes its process. This developmental process is the context for understanding adolescent satanism.

Satanism as it is expressed and experienced by teens has to do with needs that young people have—needs that are heightened by developmental changes. Their capacity to cope in healthy ways with these needs depends upon many factors: the "foundations" provided in infancy to deal with separation and loss or other relationship changes; the young person's own individual gifts and abilities; the family and other relational environments (such as church/synagogue networks, community and neighborhood support); and other environmental factors. Satanism is one option available to some teens coping with the many adolescent changes.

Table 1 on the following page lists five key developmental issues of youth in the left column. The right column suggests aspects of satanic ideology that attracts many young people. The following chapter will examine each of these issues and its collision with satanism.

Table 1

# Developmental Issues and Satanism

|  The Issue: | Aspects of Satanism  |
| --- | --- |
| **Identity**<br><br>Establishing a sense of self that is separate from others, yet still connected to them; combining the "ideal self" and "actual self"; self-consciousness and self-preoccupation occur as a result of development of a "third person perspective." | Separation achieved through the negation of others; projection of the "shadow self" outside of self; dealing with negative aspects of one's self either through such projection, or by reversal ("Bad becomes good"; "You are the center of the universe" ideology). |
| **Authority**<br><br>Natural rebellion against external and parental authority; efforts to internalize moral authority. | Support for acting out and extreme rebellion against traditional authority; encouragement to defy social and moral norms for the sake of defiance. |
| **Sexuality**<br><br>Heightened awareness of sexuality; experimenting with behaviors, boundaries, and forms of intimacy; establishing a sense of one's own self as sexual; developing an ethic for one's sexual choices. | Emphasis on sexual "freedom" as a primary aspect of self-gratification; encouragement to defy conventional norms related to appropriate sexual behavior; support for abusive treatment of others, especially women, in the name of pleasure. |
| **Belonging**<br><br>Adolescence as a peer-centered culture; self-esteem strongly related to peer acceptance; establishment of strong peer group identity partially accomplished through process of exclusion; peer group provides natural network of new attachments beyond family necessary for growth; new emotional capacities called for as teen deals with losses. | Offers the opportunity to be part of an intimate "in" group that is identifiable; peer acceptance comes through participation in group behaviors, dress, and rituals; effectively excludes others through fear. |
| **Spirituality**<br><br>Abstract thought means able to consider questions of meaning and abstraction (God, love, evil) in new ways, leading to the need for less concrete and less literal religious expression; use of symbols and ritual becomes important; experiential faith based in relationships with significant persons; highly idealistic, with potential to turn idealism into social concern. | Provides framework for spiritual expression that is highly visual and imaginative, gives youth hands-on contact with ritual; makes few requirements and includes little expectation for incorporating responsibility into beliefs; does not require intellectual work of forming a world view. |

## Chapter 4

## THE APPEAL OF ADOLESCENT SATANISM

*Blessed are the strong, for they shall possess the earth—*
*Cursed are the weak, for they shall inherit the yoke!*

*Blessed are the powerful, for they shall be reverenced*
*among men—Cursed are the feeble, for they shall be*
*blotted out!*

*Blessed are the bold, for they shall be masters of the*
*world—Cursed are the righteously humble, for they*
*shall be trodden under cloven hooves!...*

*Blessed are the death-defiant, for their days shall be*
*long in the land—Cursed are the gazers toward a*
*richer life beyond the grave, for they shall perish amidst*
*plenty!...*
—from *The Satanic Bible*[1]

This excerpt from *The Satanic Bible* provides some clues as to
the attraction of satanic ideology for youth. Does the form of the
above statements appear vaguely familiar? It may seem familiar
because it mirrors a well-known section of the Christian Bible
called the Beatitudes. Each beatitude begins with the phrase,

"Blessed are...": Blessed are the poor in spirit, for theirs is the kingdom of heaven. Blessed are the meek for they will inherit the earth....Blessed are the merciful, for they will receive mercy....Blessed are you when people revile you and persecute you and utter all kinds of evil against you falsely on my account. Rejoice and be glad for your reward is great in heaven..." (Matthew 5: 3-12). [2]

Like the beatitudes in the Book of Matthew (the first book of the New Testament) the "Satanic beatitudes" appear in section five of the first "book" of the Satanic Bible . They are a stylized reversal of the Christian Beatitudes, mimicking the language and form but with a completely opposite content. Teens struggling against their parents' traditional religion like the "Satanic beatitudes" because they mock the Bible.

Why is satanism appealing to teenagers? And why is it appealing to some teens and not to others? Let us consider some elements of satanism to which adolescents are drawn.

## Issues of Identity and Satanism

The process of developing a sense of self requires young people to do some things that help differentiate themselves from family, from the self of childhood, and even from certain peers. In these *Satanic Bible* passages, we can see how they might appeal to a teen looking to establish a unique identity. These passages stand against and even make fun of established religious writings that may be valued by parents. A young person who claims this satanic ideology is stating, "I am different from my parent, different than what their church says I should be, different from the conventional norms of religion, and different than I was as a kid."

In the quest for identity, a young person goes through many experimentations. The identity taking shape is fragile. Satanism provides protections against this fragile feeling and the threat of identity loss, strengthening their sense of self through the negation of others. Chris, a fifteen-year-old in chemical dependency treatment, spoke of a belief he shared with peers involved in a satanic group: anyone getting in the way of one's own wishes deserves retribution.

"That person becomes the enemy," he said, "and we all focus dark energy toward someone like that who is a problem. One time this friend of mine got mad at a teacher, and so our whole group did a ceremony. Nothing happened to him yet, but he really deserves it—he hassled my friend."

When asked what the teacher had done to upset his friend, Chris said that this teacher was critical of music his friend liked. As we talked further, it became evident that Chris and his group of friends experienced the teacher's critique as a criticism against their identity. The way to deal with the critique, perceived as a threat to identity, was not only to negate the teacher's perspective, but also to "negate the teacher" through a group ceremony intended to bring retribution or harm.

Young people find support for such thinking in satanic writings that speak of retributions against enemies and destruction of those who cause trouble or hardship for the satanist. A chapter in *The Satanic Bible* entitled "*On the Choice of a Human Sacrifice*".[3] makes it clear that religious satanists (i.e., members of the Church of Satan) do not condone the killing of people or animals. But the subtlety of the distinction between symbolic sacrifice (which might result in the "destruction" of the person) and actual sacrifice of animals, babies, or people (which is not condoned in these writings), seems to be lost on teens who believe that troublesome people can simply be disposed of through ritual. One way of forming identity is to learn how to cope with threats (actual and perceived) to one's sense of self. Satanic ideology appeals to youth who seek to protect their emerging and fragile sense of self through negation of others.

In what other ways do adolescent identity issues coincide with satanic ideology? For adolescents, the ability to deal with one's own imperfections is a major part of establishing a healthy self-concept. They have to figure out what to do with the aspects of who they are that fail, make mistakes, or hurt others. This can be an especially difficult problem for a person who learned as a child that "you are only loved/valued if you are 'good'." These teens find in satanism a way to project outside of themselves those parts of the self they cannot embrace, the "shadow side" of the self. Instead of admitting failure, it can be attributed to Satan! Another way to deal with failure is through reversal: "the bad becomes good." Instead of understanding harm to another person as a problem, satanic thought re-figures it as an aspect of self-gratification. Now it becomes a "positive" value and can be more easily accepted.

A complete self-concept includes the ideal and the actual self, and works to deal with the "shadow side" of the self that is so hard to accept. Many teens and adults prefer to say, *"That's not me! I'm not like that!"* when confronted with some failure, mistake, or wrongdoing. Satanism provides teens having trouble integrating this aspect of themselves with a way to locate it outside. "Satan is responsible for what I do that is wrong. He works as a channel for evil in me," reported one young man.

## The Issue of Authority and Satanism

The oppositional quality of satanism appeals to the natural needs of youth because it helps them differentiate themselves from family and other adults. It does so in a clever way that teens appreciate by mocking the familiar writings and rituals of Christianity. Satanism also dovetails with normal adolescent rebellion.

Teenagers can be quite clear that they do not want anyone else telling them what to do! They test the boundaries set for them by parents, law makers, teachers, and religious authorities. Adolescents increasingly seek to set boundaries for themselves to gain greater freedom. A teen may test the "boundary", that during the day, the school determines what is to be a good use of the teen's time, by skipping classes. This testing is part of the process of gaining the ability to be one's own determiner of how to spend a day. The need to struggle against those who represent authority is a natural aspect of growing up.

For some young people, the issue of authority becomes especially problematic. Their testing of boundaries and rebellion takes an extreme turn toward negative acting out, encouraged and supported by self-indulgent satanic ideology. The oppositional character of satanism appeals directly to a teenager's need to rebel against some of the given norms and values.

Kathy, a young adolescent from a suburban neighborhood, was part of a loosely configured group of junior high students who liked to use alcohol together and then commit petty acts of vandalism. At some point, someone in the group began to attach satanic meaning to their activities. Soon Kathy and this small group "believed" that they had a mandate from Satan to spray paint satanic symbols on church signs, sidewalks, and school doors. This group found support for its chosen way of acting out and rebelling by attaching satanic meaning to its activity.

When Kathy looked to satanic writings, she found encouragement for what they were doing. Her peer group's version of satanism gave meaning to their acts of defiance by relating that behavior to satanism. In that sense, satanism becomes the new source of authority.

What gives authority to a person in a teenager's life? In the earlier chapter on adolescent development, we noted the way authority becomes legitimate through relationships for teens— through some connection that imparts loyalty (e.g., ethnic ties), or by virtue of peer group approval. But at some point most adolescents also begin to evaluate adults using the category of *consistency* to determine whether a particular adult has a legitimate claim to authority in that teen's life. A parent who is known to steal from her office quickly loses legitimacy as one able to impose a value against teenage shoplifting. There is a loss of the "givenness" of earlier parental authority ("Because I said so") in the adolescent years.

Satanism plays into this natural developmental process by critiquing inconsistent religious practices, and by pointing to the inconsistencies between ideals and actual behaviors of persons. With their heightened idealism, teenagers are especially sensitive to hypocrisy. For some young people, the awareness of parental fallibility and inconsistency marks the end of their willingness to view their parents or others as legitimate authorities in their lives. Satanism encourages the rejection of persons in traditional positions of authority by virtue of their inevitable inconsistency—manifested in the inability to perfectly live up to what they teach.

If external sources of decision-making and authority become less legitimate for teens, what replaces them? The normal developmental movement is toward vesting authority in the peer group. But eventually a person moves toward a more internal sense of authority, one that comes from within the self. Although this movement continues beyond adolescent years, these years see significant steps toward its occurrence. A teen who uses satanism to "bypass" the struggle with authority moves into young adulthood with a handicap.

One important aspect of locating the "control center" for decision-making and ethical thinking inside the self rather than in the environment (rules, parents, or peer) is the ability to delay gratification—to put off the experience of pleasure for the sake of a greater good or for later gratification. A person who is unable to decide from within themselves when it might be better or more appropriate to delay a gratifying experience must rely on external sources such as rules to guide their behavior.

Satanic writings seize on those religious perspectives that teach some form of delayed gratification and treat them as the mainstream of Judeo-Christian moral teaching. Sources such as *The Satanic Bible* proceed as if the whole of Judeo-Christian moral teaching could be summed up in the following phrase: If you enjoy doing something, it's wrong—and if you avoid doing the things you most enjoy now, then you will be rewarded in heaven for denying yourself. The statement quoted at the beginning of this chapter, "Cursed are the gazers toward a richer life beyond the grave, for they shall perish amidst plenty!" is one disdainful satanic expression concerning self-denial.

Unfortunately, one of the abuses of Christian theology has been an unhealthy exalting of self-denial for its own sake. Some people of faith have shown a tendency to value the act of denying the self above any greater good which an act might accomplish. "Going without" becomes more important than "going without a new car" which would allow a child in the family to attend college. It is this sort of attitude—self-denial for its own sake—that is attacked in satanic ideology. But satanism's answer to such an abuse is to reject the value of being able to delay gratification. Persons receive encouragement to indulge themselves in whatever they desire; putting off one's own pleasure for the sake of someone else is viewed as false charity.

Compared to their childhood, adolescents show marked increase in their ability to delay gratification. But they are also notoriously impulsive. In satanism, some teens find the support to act upon the immediacy of their feelings and desired without concern for the consequences. The "authority" for their actions is not in some law or parental rule, nor is it really located within themselves. The authority for their actions rests in what they want to do in a given moment. For young people having difficulty delaying gratification, satanism offers a solution by ridiculing those who do not indulge their immediate desire.

## Sexuality and Satanism

Before social scientists were aware of the developmental period known as adolescence, before physicians could delineate the exact nature of physical changes occurring during that period, ancient peoples had knowledge of a sexually mature age. Most societies created rituals to mark the event, and established norms to guide or regulate sexual behavior. It did not require science or medicine to figure out that at a certain point in a young person's growth, sexuality came into prominence in ways that bought both celebration and problems. And even though we possess the capacity to understand sexual maturation medically and socially, we have not moved beyond ancient cultures in our ability to hold together sexuality in both its celebrative and problematic dimensions.

Much of the reputation of the Church of Satan, and a good deal of the media attention received by reportedly satanic groups around the country, center on its ideology of free sexual expression. For adolescents experiencing a time of heightened sexual awareness, it is natural and even important for them to experiment with behaviors, new boundaries in relationships, and new forms of intimacy related to sexual feelings. When this experimentation happens within acceptable norms of the family and community, it can be no big deal, even though the emotional ups and downs of adolescent sexual intimacy seem difficult for teens in the best of situations.

One major reason for the difficulty concerns the link between sexual intimacy and a new kind of rejection. Most of the time, healthy teens are able to weather the stormy ups and downs of forming and losing romantic attachments with undue duress. This doesn't mean they have no trouble. But most of the time, teens cope with the rollercoaster of "crushes" and falling in and out of love. In the process, they learn how to deal with the multitude of feelings connected to romantic intimacy. For some young people, however, the experimentation, the possibilities for romantic rejection, and the need to develop some form of personal ethic to guide sexual behaviors become the occasion for some unhealthy or negative developments. Satanic ideology may become appealing in several ways: it affirms and encourages them to act on their sexual feelings; it offers a ready-made ethic; it dispenses with shame and guilt; and it offers a solution to the problem of rejection.

Satanic writings used by adolescents are filled with sexual language and affirmation for acting on whatever sexual feelings and fantasies give pleasure. Such writings can be very enticing and titillating to adolescent readers with heightened awareness of sexual feelings. Recall from Chapter 1 the description of the "altar" for the Black Mass—"a nude woman." Or consider the following sample of the highly sexualized language of *The Satanic Bible*: "Concerning sex or lust: Take full advantage of spells and charms that work; if you be a man, plunge your erect member into her with lascivious delight; if you be a woman, open wide your loins in lewd anticipation." [4] Both examples appear theatrical, but to an adolescent dealing with strong sexual feelings and low self-esteem, such sexualized contents make satanism attractive.

Much of the sexual satanic language involves domination along with objectification of others. Such a focus provides a mechanism for some teens, particularly young men, to combat fears of rejection through notions of domination over a sex partner. Should one be hurt or rejected by another person, themes of retribution offer a way to deal with their vulnerability.

The encouragement to act on sexual feelings in defiance of commonly held norms appeals to the natural rebellious inclinations of teens who seek ways to differentiate themselves from their families or from "the establishment."

Jason, a teenager who had participated in satanic rituals over a period of several months with some friends, was dealing with his troubled family relationships in treatment. He came from a family that did not speak openly about sexual issues. Through this silence came the message that "sex is a bad thing." Jason struggled against this unspoken norm.

"I think about sex all the time," he said. " I don't believe that people should have to wait until they get married to have sex. My mom and dad are so uptight and old-fashioned."

Asked about how he resolved the dilemma between his own strong sexual feelings and rigid family values, he replied: "The Bible teaches people that sex is bad, but *The Satanic Bible* says that sex is good. So I decided to go by *The Satanic Bible*. It's great—you can do whatever you want to."

Jason's statement points to both the failure of church communities to communicate a positive sense of sexuality to youth, and to the appeal of satanism's focus on sexual expression as a vital form of self-gratification.

## Issues of Belonging and Satanism

The journey from infancy to adulthood is like a series of concentric circles, representing the expanding world of human connections and personal experiences. A baby's initial world centers around parents. Gradually this world expands to include siblings and other family members such as grandparents, aunts, and uncles. A new "ring" is added as new experiences (child care, nursery school, church or synagogue) bring other significant adults (and some children) into the child's life. Later, playmates and classmates become especially important.

For adolescents, the need to re-negotiate attachments within the family, and to differentiate from parents happens in part through a sort of "transfer" of attachment energy from parents to peers. It becomes less difficult to achieve some degree of separation (psychologically) if a person has others with whom to form attachments. So peer attachments take on heightened developmental significance. And self-esteem frequently becomes closely related to peer acceptance during adolescence.

What about young people who have a difficult time relating to a peer group, or for some reason never quite feel as though they belong? Many of these young people know a pervasive sense of loneliness. Some are able to cope with it by finding support from adults with whom they relate more easily than their own peers. Others pour themselves into activities such as sports or music in an effort to fill the void. Today, many teens turn to chemicals as a way to deal with loneliness.

For a teen without a sense of belonging to a group, nagging questions of "What's wrong with me?" begin to pull on self-esteem. But satanism gives a feeling of being part of a close-knit "in" group. And for teens, with their "imaginary audience" and self-consciousness about how others perceive them, a good part of the issue is whether *other people* see them as belonging. For those adolescents whose expression of satanism takes visible forms such as wearing symbols or particular clothing, being identified by others as part of a group gives a sense of belonging.

For the adolescent who may feel "unworthy" or unable to belong to other peer groups, satanism offers a relatively low admission standard. The only thing a young person need do to belong is to participate in group activities.

J. Gordon Melton notes that although it is difficult to say how widespread the occurrence of adolescent satanism is, it is most prevalent in the "gang scene" in Southern California. He also observes that teen satanism has spread through racist groups such as the "skinheads" or the "Aryan Resistance". Public efforts to decimate gangs tends to disrupt adolescent satanism as well. [5] The parallels between youth gang involvement and teen satanism reflect a similar underlying dynamic: the search for a community of belonging, attained through negative means.

One way people establish group membership is through exclusion: establishing which groups or people they are *not* connected with further affirms those places where they find belonging. In adolescence, such exclusion frequently manifests itself as "cliques", small clannish groups of teens. Being on the outside of one of these groups can be extremely painful for teens, particularly when the group includes childhood friends.

When an unidentifiable group exists, satanism functions to strengthen the young person's sense of belonging by virtue of who is excluded. There is a secrecy, a sense of specialness because only certain people belong to this group. In some instances the "exclusion factor" is powerful, and teens identified with satanism see school peers or adults respond with fear. "We know something they don't know" increases belonging by deepening the distance between those who claim a connection to satanism and those who are outsiders.

In a halfway house following primary chemical dependency treatment, a group of residents construct a Ouija board. They use it to "contact the spirits" and "get the power to throw a curse on the counselors". These quotes come from Ann, one young woman who labeled the group's actions as satanic, because "we would call on Satan to take us to the Gates of Hell so we could contact the dead."

Ann said that she was not sure she believed in the reality of everything the group did or said. Yet she liked it because "we were together and nobody else bothered us. They knew we could put a curse or something on them and they were afraid. Sometimes I even got afraid, and I was one of the ones doing it!" Ann's reflections reveal the importance of a sense of belonging, a quality that is partially generated through the exclusion of others.

To talk about issues of belonging as they relate to satanism may suggest that adolescent satanism involves many established groups. Certainly the popular view of teen satanism is an organized nationwide system with which youth affiliate, often after being coerced into them by adults. There is no evidence for such a view. Satanic involvement concerns the young person's own experience of being part of a group. Adolescents commonly identify themselves as "part of a satanic group" or as being "Satan worshipers" on the basis of a one-time participation in some gathering or ritual with a few peers. These teens are not actually a part of any established, organized group. But they *experience* themselves as being a part of a group. They feel a sense of belonging.

## Issues of Spirituality and Satanism

The life stage of adolescence opens new opportunities for spiritual development. Some persons, accustomed to thinking about spirituality in more static terms, may wonder at the idea that humans develop spiritually. And yet it makes sense that a four-year-old does not have the same understanding of God as a forty-year-old. The adult has conceptual abilities, experiences, and relationships far beyond those of the four-year-old, all of which affect the understanding of God. Our spirituality grows as we do. Just as people experience emotional or intellectual growth, human spirituality is a changing, moving phenomenon.

Abstract thought by teens has important implications for spiritual development. The ability to conceptualize abstractly allows new ways of considering questions of meaning or transcendence. "What is the purpose of my life?" "How can a Higher Power be part of me but more than me at the same time?" These kinds of questions take on new levels of meaning. A child might think, "What is the purpose of my life?" in terms of what she plans to do today. In contrast, a teen may think about life as bigger than or transcending today's activities. Life is an entity itself.

The shift from concrete thinking toward abstract thinking ability leads to the need by youth for a less literal religious or spiritual expression than the spirituality of their childhood. For example, there is now the option of the young person to understand the story of Noah's Ark as both an event and as a symbol for multiple meanings (God's loving plan for the creation, or an ark as a symbol for safety amidst a storm). For teens, symbols are no longer limited to a one-to-one correspondence with the realities they represent.

Everyone enjoys practicing a new skill in which they show some ability. Teens are no exception. They enjoy practicing and developing their new found skill at using metaphors and symbols to express multiple meanings. And so the use of ritual becomes significant, as an arena for practicing their skill. All people employ ritual in their lives. All of us use patterns for ordering our activities. Some people wake up at the same time each day and go through a certain order of activities (make coffee, brush teeth, wake up the kids, pack a lunch). Some ritual, particularly religious ritual, involves a patterned use of symbol, story, and metaphor, both to "make meaning" and to express meaning.

Adolescents enjoy employing ritual because it is a way to express themselves. But it is important that the patterns of action and symbols used be "alive"—really meaningful. The satanism of *The Satanic Bible* becomes a source for the symbols and imagery of adolescent satanism. Much of this imagery relies on the nature-related symbols of air, fire, earth, and water. They appeal to the adolescent's notion of "being natural". "I like the way satanism is more natural—instead of being fake," said David. "I mean, like it talks about power in the earth and fire. They're things I can see. Did you ever see a 'holy ghost'? I like doing what's natural. Sex is a natural thing. So is getting back at people who screw you over—it's a natural instinct to want revenge. Satanism is like that, you know. It tells you to be natural and real. People are really just another kind of animal, so we should do what comes natural and not try to censor it. Satan stands for all that."

Given the importance of establishing a unique identity and differentiating themselves from parents, teens often want to separate themselves from the rituals and means of spiritual expression used by their family. They like "doing our own worship service" as part of a church youth group where the group can create its own patterns of symbol use. Or they will attend a church service, but sit together in the back row rather than with their families. Some adults perceive the rejection shown by some teens of "established religion" or "adult church" as the young person's rejection of God, faith, or spiritual experience. These events more accurately reflect the teen's need and desire to begin a new level of identifying their own symbols of faith and their own experience of God.

Adolescent faith is an experiential spirituality based on relationships with significant people—peers, adults, role models, heroes and heroines. It is a spirituality in the process of integration, as youth work to integrate their various ideas, questions, and experiences into a world view. It is a questioning, doubting, searching time, requiring considerable work. There is the potential during adolescence for idealism to be translated into social concern—as when young people, concerned about the environment, begin a recycling campaign in their school. There also exists the potential for their idealism to translate into cynical thoughts or self-centeredness.

Satanism plays on the potential for cynicism and self-centeredness in young people. Instead of encouraging them to turn idealism outside of themselves, into action that benefits others and themselves, satanic philosophy offers a cynical fatalism: this is it; lofty ideas about making the world a better place or doing something for someone else are really only disguised efforts at self-elevation.

Satanism does not require much of young people to develop a world view out of one's beliefs, questions, doubts, and experiences. It does not require them to think or feel deeply about anything beyond themselves. Instead it offers a way to make a complex world more manageable with its dramatic glorification of the power of evil. Evil, pain and injustice are difficult issues to sort through, and they make the task of developing a world view quite complex. Satanism simplifies this for teens. Instead of coming to grips with destruction and chaotic experiences, satanism lifts up such experiences as that to which a person aspires, exemplified in the figure of Satan.

Many young people greet the expanding horizons of their world and their increasingly expansive thinking abilities with delight. But for other youth, such expansion means trouble. It is the equivalent of over-stimulation: the young person faces new challenges and possibilities but lacks the resources to deal with them and so becomes overwhelmed. For these young people, the language and ideas in satanic writings may be especially appealing. At the same time that these writings appeal to newly developing language and thinking skills, they protect teens from too great a stretch. They offer teens a way to compartmentalize issues. Satanism also allows teens to maintain a black-and-white separation of good and evil, and avoid struggling with the many gray areas of ambiguity. And the hard work of moral growth during adolescence and young adulthood is entirely negated by satanism. The only important ethic or value is the priority of the self.

An earlier chapter described satanism as a phenomenon of adolescent development with religious or spiritual overtones. While it is not primarily a religious or spiritual experience of the adolescents who identify with satanism, their involvement and attraction to satanism has an effect on their spirituality, and is related to spiritual needs. Satanism appeals to young people by providing a framework for expression of "things of another world" that is highly visual and imaginative. At the same time as the visual aspects of satanism reach back to a more concrete expression of meaning, its imaginative aspects draw on the young person's new abilities to construe reality in abstract ways.

Black candles, used by some teens in their satanic rituals, have specific meanings attached to their color and use—meanings that teenagers know about and can articulate. This stands in contrast to the situation in many American church communities where the candle color is selected to match the sanctuary carpet, and carries no particular symbolic or ritual meaning. The intrigue of having personal access to ritual meanings and symbolism is a powerful attraction when the surrounding religious landscape either appears devoid of all symbols or uses symbols randomly.

In addition, the visual dimensions of satanic ritual, as impromptu and unplanned as they may be, make them especially attractive to certain populations of youth, such as hearing impaired teens. Some chemical dependency counselors of hearing impaired youth speculate that satanism occurs more frequently among their clients precisely because of its strongly visual dimension. Other young people who process information visually instead of through hearing or reading will also find the strong visual aspects of satanic ritual appealing.

### Emotions and the Spirituality of Teens

Although one might not be able to tell it from sitting in some contemporary religious services, spirituality is not only a thinking affair. It also involves feelings, passions, and emotions. This suggests a major reason satanism appeals to some teens: satanism legitimizes anger and its expressions, even in destructive and violent ways. Many young people hear from traditional faith communities that anger is incompatible with belief. With satanism, acting out of anger is encouraged in the form of retribution against "enemies." "The mighty voices of my vengeance smash the stillness of the air and stand as monoliths of wrath...I call upon the messengers of doom to slash with grim delight this victim I hath chosen" [6] ; or "Hate your enemies with a whole heart, and if a man smite you on one cheek, SMASH him on the other!" [7]

Teens experience strong, volatile emotions that may include rage. Young people who have been physically or sexually abused, or who have known the intensified powerlessness of poverty, racism, or sexism, understandably carry within them a great deal of anger. There is no sense to them in taking on a spirituality that bans this anger. When satanism appears to be a spirituality that endorses the display of anger, it speaks to the needs of these youths.

One adolescent described his connection with satanism this way: "It's not like I really cared about Satan or worshipped the Devil—but I wanted to do the opposite of the church. Church is a place where you sit and you have to shut up all the time. I wanted to be where I could scream or hit somebody if I felt like it. I didn't get into the ceremonies so much—I guess I don't really believe, ya know, deep inside—I just used them (the satanic ceremonies) as a place to curse and yell and be mad."

## Putting the Pieces Together

This chapter began with the question, "Why is satanism appealing to adolescents?" Some adolescents would find nothing appealing about satanism. For them, it is a neutral affair, to which they are neither drawn nor repelled. To others, its content, the way it mocks Christianity, and its association with illicit activity go beyond simply being uninteresting or unappealing. To this group of young people, satanism is offensive. It stands against their values or beliefs.

But for some teens, satanism holds great attraction. Who are these teens, and what distinguishes them from the other two groups who do not find satanism attractive?

It is not enough to say that adolescent satanism relates to the issues encountered by teens as they grow up. Teens in all three groups encounter these same issues. Teens attracted to satanism have difficulty negotiating the issues and transitions that are normal to adolescence. For this group of young people, satanism becomes a way to manage the issues of identity, authority, sexuality, belonging, and spirituality, when other ways of coping have either failed or not been available.

### Some Cope Better Than Others . . . Sometimes

The chart on the next page suggests a "coping scale," or a range of ease and comfort with which adolescents weather the transitions of growth. Coping is a word that refers to a person's ability to adapt to change, transition, and stress. All of us have varying abilities to cope with the different life transitions we encounter. And even within one individual, the ability to cope may be situational—it depends on the specific issue at hand. A friend of mine who is a single parent says that she does not have trouble dealing with the need to find reliable child care on a regular basis. Other situations, however, cause her great difficulty and tend to exhaust her emotional resources: getting bills paid on time, or arranging transportation to hockey practice for her son. She seems to bring different internal strengths and external resources to the situation of finding child care than to these latter situations.

79

## Coping Scale

**High Functioning**

**Low Functioning**

| Coping Well | Adequately Coping | Moderately Coping | Marginally Coping |
|---|---|---|---|
| A variety of daily activities, multiple relationships, and claims on one's energies are well-managed. | Daily routine is comfortable; minor stresses managed appropriately. | Change in routine may trigger stress disproportionate to the situation; adaption to stress requires "borrowing energy" from other areas of life (academics, peer relationships). | Daily life lacks structure; situations responded to randomly, dependent on available energies; adaptive capacities bound up in survival. |

Similarly, an adolescent may cope extremely well with the ups and downs of peer group changes and cliques (inclusion and exclusion) that accompany the teen years. But the same young person who manages these issues of belonging so well may have considerably more trouble adapting to changes of physical growth or sexual development. And yet there is a level of overall coping ability that distinguishes some teens from others. If a young person has some basic sense of competency coping in one area of life, that in itself is a strength for meeting and adapting to difficulty or change in other life areas.

No one plans *not* to have coping skills! People do not simply wake up one day and decide whether or not they will be able to adapt to the transitions and stresses that come their way. The ability to cope effectively with change depends on more than individual constitution. It also involves environmental factors, ethnic upbringing, personal history, resources, and the intensity and number of stressors being experienced.

Some adolescents adapt amazingly well to the many transitions in the teen years. While no one copes perfectly with every situation, these teens are located closer to the HIGH FUNCTIONING/COPING WELL end of the chart. When confronted with a challenge or difficulty, they can mobilize a variety of resources to help deal with the challenge.

Internal resources, like a healthy self-esteem, allow these young people to handle losing a game, receiving a poor grade, or feeling rejected by a friend or romantic interest. Their entire sense of worth is not invested in the game, the grade, or the person rejecting them. Even though there probably will be a temporary period of "imbalance," youths who fall into this category can rely on their healthy self-esteem to help them adjust. Other internal resources, those found within the young person, include personality factors like friendliness, intelligence, or particular skills such as musical or leadership abilities.

In the chapter on adolescent development, we looked at the way that infants mature, and the various obstacles they must overcome as they make their way toward a separate sense of self. An important key to the internal resources of a teenager may be found in the experiences of infancy and early childhood. It is common, for example, to see adolescents who experienced the loss of a parent during infancy carrying deep-seated fears of abandonment that resurface during adolescence. An infant who did not experience consistent and reliable child care may internalize fears: "It's not OK to go out there and try new things. If I separate from mom, she won't be there when I come back." Although this happens as a pre-verbal, inner psychological dynamic, it has the power to affect how that person feels about her/himself—especially when, as a teen, the issues of growing up closely mirror those of infancy. Internal resources relate in this way to personal history, especially to the experiences of early attachment and separation with parents.

External resources include relationships with people as well as non-human factors in the environment. A generally positive and open relationship with parents is frequently cited by teens as one of the most important resources available to them, or as a resource they wish they had. The atmosphere within the family—supportive or chaotic—affects a teens' coping abilities. A supportive and caring family environment offers an important external resource for youth.

Other external resources are a positive school environment; supportive same-age friends; involvement in planned, organized activities such as band, church youth group, or swim team; and the availability of adults other than parents who act in caring and affirming ways. When confronted with a challenge or difficulty, they can mobilize a variety of resources to help deal with the challenge.

Moving along the coping scale, there are some teens whose ability to cope is ADEQUATE. They have enough resources, both internal and external, to adjust to the changes and stress of adolescence. But there seems to be a bit more struggle or difficulty as they make these adjustments. An example is the teen who adjusts to the divorce of her parents gradually, managing to keep her grades and activities going after an initial slump, but then experiences a low-level depression over a period of time. While she is adjusting adequately to the changes in her family situation, she does so with some difficulty or struggle. In many cases, such struggle is entirely appropriate. There are times when adaptation to stress is actually more harmful than helpful—if the adjustment inhibits the ability to cope with stress.

Young people who adapt or become accustomed to stress may actually be putting themselves in danger. Teens who grow accustomed to violence in the home may not notice the real danger in which they live. Sometimes, then, a teen who is "adequately coping" with a problem such as chaotic home life exhibits a healthier, more functional response than "high-functioning" teens because the coping does not mask the need for change in the home environment. It simply allows the teen to deal with stress.

Still other teens find themselves only somewhat able to adapt to change, perhaps depending on the nature of difficulty, or perhaps related to a "changeable" resource such as the presence of non-parental adults who may move away or fail to stay involved with a teen. These teens are identified as MODERATELY COPING. It may be that environmental factors like poverty or the absence of parental support limit their coping ability. But they have some internal coping strengths to fall back on. However, those same internal resources may not get them through in all situations.

Consider the teen who manages to deal with issues of belonging by joining a band. Even though his friends from junior high have formed their own group and are ignoring him, he adapts to this by joining another group. He has some ability with music and is moderately outgoing, so the adaptation to a new peer group is not overly difficult. But when his girlfriend tells him that she wants to break up, he goes through a period of intense anger and acting out, vandalizing cars and school buildings. Eventually he manages to adjust—and even finds a new girlfriend. But he remains deeply "wounded" from the experience, and it continues to affect his self-esteem as well as his relationships with young women.

The last group of teens on the coping continuum are those for whom stressors have been too great, internal and external resources are insufficient, or both . When a person, teen or adult, is unable to adapt to a transition or stressor, and can neither avoid the transition nor eliminate the stress, a state of dysfunction results. In the presence of great stress and few resources, teens usually resort to extreme or negative options. These teens are MARGINALLY COPING. They are just barely managing, and the ability to do even that may depend on some extremely dysfunctional survival behaviors.

A marginally coping teen is someone who begins to use alcohol to numb her feelings of pain from the sexual abuse she has experienced; the young person who begins to carve on her arms to obtain some small measure of relief from the intense inner pain she cannot express; the adopted young man who acts abusively toward women in response to feelings of maternal abandonment; the young man who feels compelled to challenge every authority figure he encounters with threatening postures, gestures, language or even violence. In each of these situations, the young person involved is surviving, functioning, managing to make it to the next day. But the ability to cope, even marginally, comes at the price of great self-destruction and sometimes even harm to another.

Sometimes in America's individualistic, "pull yourself up by your own bootstraps" culture there emerges a tendency to blame people for not coping well. It is well known that economics, race, and gender, along with the experiences of personal history (such as adoption, or abuse) bear a strong relationship to a young person's style and ability to cope. These factors comprise some of the "givens" of a person's situation. They are not chosen by the person. But they sometimes make all the difference in the world when it comes to coping with stress.

## The Shaping of Coping Styles

An experiment offering a choice to groups of suburban youth and groups of urban youth yielded different results. When offered the chance to have a single candy bar now, or to wait several days to receive five candy bars middle class suburban teens most often chose to wait and receive more candy. Their experiences have taught them that it pays to wait and that one can trust a person in authority to do what they said they would. Young people from the inner city whose experiences of poverty and racism taught them that what really matters is what they have now because one cannot trust that someone will follow through on a promise, tended to take the one candy bar.

The same attitudes and experiences informing these choices also affect the ways of coping. Personal history and experience, including the experience of race or class barrier, affect the style and choices a person makes to adapt to a situation. What appears to be highly dysfunctional for one person may be an important act of coping for another. The diagram on coping styles is not intended to suggest that all cultural groups can or should cope with stress in the same way. It does suggest, however, that within the limits of one's environment and the "givens" of a person's existence such as race and gender, there exists a range of ability to adapt.

### Satanism: Who's At Risk?

Teenagers today experience multiple stressors. There are the inherent transitions of adolescent development, particularly in the areas of identity, authority, sexuality, belonging and spirituality. Issues related to each of these five areas brings a certain level of stress into the lives of adolescents because they require the young person to adapt to changes. But adolescents also must deal with increasingly intense stressors and changes beyond the natural, developmental ones: parental divorce or job change, the death or suicide of a friend, pressures to succeed from a very early age, frequent moves and the loss of community roots, decisions about using drugs, and the presence of dangerous and even deadly sexually transmitted diseases such as AIDS. In a group of ten teens I spoke with recently, five had lost at least one friend in a car crash involving a drunk driver. Two had school acquaintances who died by suicide. And one had just recently learned that her best friend has cancer. These young people were not in a treatment setting, where one might easily rationalize by saying, "They are troubled, so they know more friends who are troubled too, and therefore are more likely to be suicidal or drinking while driving." This was an average group of teens. The harsh reality today is that many young people have to deal with significant losses and deaths—even people their own age. It seems as if their lives are more stressful because life is more stressful.

Adolescent satanism appears when teenagers have difficulty negotiating the transitions and stresses of their lives. Young people who experience problems dealing with changing relationships and attachments to adolescence and who also have fewer internal and external resources to help them cope with the changes may discover that satanism meets the needs they feel most immediately. In other words, young people most at risk for involvement in satanism are those whom we would locate closer to the "marginally coping" end of the scale.

Do youth who are coping well with the stresses of life and who appear to have plenty of support in the form of parental and community resources ever find satanism attractive? Of course they do. Young people with good coping skills and adequate resources share the same curiosity about the occult as do youths with poorer coping skills and fewer resources. The difference is that the young person who is functioning well is less likely to discover in satanism a new and intriguing way for unmet needs to be addressed. That young person has other ways that work much better than satanism. While satanism may be quite interesting to them it does not offer the kind of lifeline it appears to be for those youth on the poorly coping/high stress/low functioning end of the scale.

## The Drug Connection

Many of the teens who are "marginally coping" include drug and alcohol use in their repertoire of coping efforts. These teens would not identify their drug use as a way to cope with pain. "I was just out to have a good time. I wanted to feel good." This is a common response by young people in the evaluation stage or early stage of treatment. "It doesn't mean anything else. I don't have feelings." For some teens, satanic activity is little more than a vehicle for using drugs. "Let's go into the woods and do a satanic ceremony" is really a poor cover for "let's go get high."

Although religious satanists like LaVey's group denounce drug use by their members as being contrary to satanic philosophy which stresses being in touch with reality, young people have seized onto the "do your own thing" pleasure-seeking aspects of satanism as justification and encouragement of their chemical use.

"I acted like I was into the Devil," acknowledged one young person, "and I did all the things like make a blood pact and promise to give my soul to the Devil in exchange for power now...but what it was for me was a cheap way to get buzzed." Many of his peers share his testimony.

The link between drug use and adolescent satanism appears to work in both directions. If young persons use drugs, they are more likely to encounter others who talk about or participate in satanic activity. If a young person is attracted to satanism and winds up with others who act on that interest through some ritual expression or behavior, most likely drugs are involved. The reason for this mutual relationship is simple: both drug use and satanism relate to a young person's search for the power to overcome difficulty, boredom, bad feelings, and the transitions of adolescence.

There is no single description or definition for "involvement in satanism". For some it is a fleeting, barely significant attraction. For others it may become criminal or dangerous. Just as young people with the fewest resources and the least ability to cope show the highest risk for satanic involvement, those youth with the fewest resources and the least ability to cope are much more likely to manifest a destructive or problematic style of participation in satanism.

## Where Do They Get the Idea?

We have emphasized repeatedly that the varieties of satanism practiced by adolescents have little if anything to do with the established "religious satanism" of the Church of Satan. This organization sees itself as promoting "the development of strong individuals who seek the greatest gratification out of life and practice selfish virtues as long as they harm no other."[8] This emphasis is not an effort to support or denigrate that group. Instead, it is an attempt to make clear these facts: adolescent satanism lacks a central organization; does not have a theology and is not a religious phenomenon. So where do adolescents practicing satanic rituals get the ideas and content for these rituals? These and other related questions will be answered in the next chapter.

# Chapter 5

## THE IDEA OF THE DEVIL

"Did you see that scary movie on TV last night?" one teen asks another as they walk down the school hall.

"Yeah," says the other. "I liked the part where that guy was walking along and all of a sudden this slimy demon hand reached up out of the ground and pulled him down into hell."

"What about the part when the woman was talking to her boyfriend—his face changed and she could see from his eyes that he was really the Devil?"

Down the hall in the lounge, a teacher begins a joke: "There was a man who died and went to heaven, but St. Peter wouldn't let him in until he got clearance from the Devil. So he went down to talk to the Devil about it. When he got there, he met three different guys in red suits..."

Meanwhile, across town at the school board building, a parent tries to get the board to ban the use of the devil symbol as a mascot or name for school sports teams. "We are talking here about a serious and evil supernatural power that should not be taken lightly."

One of the board members nods affirmatively, while another says to herself, "Oh, come on! It's the age of science. Surely this guy doesn't believe in the Devil still."

In each of these conversations people appear to be talking about the same subject, the Devil. But it is also clear that each one ascribes different meanings to the concept, and holds different beliefs about the Devil. Despite such differences in beliefs, almost anyone who grows up in the U.S. is familiar with the figure commonly known as Satan, the Devil or Lucifer. It is a common part of our culture, appearing in jokes, cartoons, movies, television, and advertising.

The diversity of ways the Devil is depicted in these media indicates a wide range of beliefs and perspectives about Satan. On one end of the spectrum of beliefs resides the benign toy-like figure of the Devil dressed in red who sports horns and a pitchfork—clearly a story book character with no religious or supernatural aspects. This depiction of Satan shows up in cartoons and advertising, especially around Halloween. A closely related view is the whimsical notion of the Devil as a mischief-maker, popularized in the 1960s by comedian Flip Wilson with his phrase, "The Devil made me do it." This smiling, mischievous depiction of the Devil is a figure in jokes about human irresponsibility, or advertisements showing someone who is tempted to indulge in a rich dessert. It is a playful picture of Satan that lacks any sense of real harm or any "diabolical" identity.

Still others view the Devil as a supernatural being who is the embodiment of evil, destruction and chaos in the world. This group includes a fairly significant part of the population. At the other end of the spectrum is the use of Satan as a metaphor to personify what is essentially a spiritual force or energy working against the good. Whatever people believe, it is clear that the Devil is part of modern American culture.

Where do we get our information about the Devil? The question would be much easier to answer if "the Devil" were an idea that stood still. But what people mean by "the Devil" is anything but fixed. The concept has changed over time, even within the religious traditions of Judaism and Christianity that offer the main theological views of Satan in this country. Regardless of whether one thinks about Satan as a supernatural entity, an actual being, a force, or a metaphor, it is still possible to acknowledge that people have viewed Satan differently in different times. Because the concept of Satan described by adolescents frequently is a blend of different understandings, it is useful to be familiar with some of the major sources in our culture for beliefs about the Devil.

## Perspectives on Satan from Religious Tradition

Ask most people where they learned whatever they know about Satan, and they will likely respond by mingling some vague Sunday School memories about fallen angels with Greek and Roman mythology about the underworld. "Doesn't it say in the Bible that Satan was an angel who tried to be greater than God, so Satan was thrown out of heaven and has been making trouble ever since?" "I always thought that Satan was put by God at the entrance of hell to guard against anyone leaving." Given most people's uncertainty about exactly where their pictures of Satan or the Devil come from, it is not surprising that teenagers also have trouble identifying the source or sources of their ideas.

## Sources in Religious Tradition for the Idea of the Devil

Every world view, philosophy, and religious movement must wrestle with the nature and source of evil. All must decide how to deal with the problem of evil and where to locate it. Does evil come from human beings? From God? Does it exist at all? The Hebrew Bible, called the Old Testament by Christians, contains writings compiled over many centuries, and reflects several developments in thinking about the problem of evil. The earlier writings of the Old Testament consider God to be the source of all things, good and evil. These writings contain no mention of the Devil or Satan. In writings from a later period the Hebrew word "Satan" appears.

### "Satan" as a Job Description

The word Satan means "opponent" or "accuser". Its initial use is not as a proper noun or name for a specific supernatural being. Instead "Satan" referred to a role that might even have been carried out by humans, that is, Satan functioned like a job title. Later the word "Satan" applied to supernatural beings who acted in God's service in their role as accusers. A "satan" was one who worked on God's behalf to accuse Israel of wrong, a kind of prosecuting attorney. This depiction of satan lacks the sense of demonic power working in opposition to the Divine, which appeared in still later writings. Then the idea of "Satan" referred to a particular supernatural being whose very nature was in opposition to God.

### *"The Devil Made Me Do It"* Version of Satan

A slightly different view of the role of Satan occurs in other Old Testament writings. These refer to Satan as one who actually incites a human to evil or wrongdoing (e.g., I Chronicles, 21:1 where David is incited by a "Satan" to go against God's commands.)[1] The book of Job shows Satan in two distinct roles: first, as Job's accuser before God, and later as the one who brings suffering and misfortune to Job.

The Christian New Testament displays a further change in the understanding of Satan, moving more towards the idea of Satan as a supernatural being opposed to God. This removes the cause of evil to a source outside of God. In the literature of the New Testament, the Devil is described as "the one who has the power of death, that is, the devil" (Hebrews 2:14)[2]; the one who tempts people or turns them away from God (Luke 4: 1ff, 8:12)[3]; and the one who caused Judas Iscariot to betray Jesus to the Roman authorities (John 13:2)[4]. Like New Testament stories of demon possession, these texts convey the belief that the Devil is one who takes people over, tempting them or causing them to act in evil ways.

The New Testament occasionally portrays Satan as the opponent of Christ. For young people who are developing a faith identity, the dichotomy between good and evil, God and Satan, takes on new interest—especially as depicted in the fantastical language of the Book of Revelation.

### Satan: A Fallen Angel?

Where did the commonly held view of Satan as a fallen angel originate? There exists a sizable body of writings that did not become a part of the Biblical canon but which nonetheless were popularly read and influenced theological thinking of Jewish and Jewish-Christian groups. Two such documents are I and II Enoch, and the Book of Jubilee. They, along with other writings, form the body of literature knows as the "Pseudepigrapha", a Greek word meaning "false writings."

Enoch is a collection of apocalyptic writing mostly dealing with evils origins, angels, and celestial bodies such as star and planets. It fits a genre of literature knows as "apocalyptic" literature. Apocalyptic writings are those documents, such as the book of Revelation in the New Testament, written out of a sense of the imminent end of the world and start of a new, messianic age. Apocalyptic literature generally comes out of a situation of great struggle and persecution, and gives expression to its writers' vision of a new reality that will punish the oppressors and reward or exalt the persecuted.

## Seven-Headed Beasts, Demons and Things That Go Bump In the Night

These imaginative scenarios portray the oppressors as beasts or demons. A quotation from Enoch appears in the New Testament letter of Jude and illustrates the kind of language common to apocalyptic material: "It was also about these that Enoch, in the seventh generation from Adam, prophesied, saying, "See, the Lord is coming with ten thousands of his holy ones, to execute judgment on all, and to convict everyone of all the deeds of ungodliness that they have committed in such an ungodly way, and of all the harsh things that ungodly sinners have spoken against him" (Jude 14-15)[5]. Apocalyptic literature is written by the persecuted "good people" about how the "bad people" are about to get their just reward.

I Enoch tells the story of a group of heavenly beings known as the "Watchers."[6] The writer of the Book of Jubilee tells the story of these watcher angels who come to Earth to teach people how they should live. But when they get there, the Watchers are overcome by sexual desire for human women. After that, says the Book of Jubilee, what they do is evil. So God sends them under the earth, but allows their leader to keep one watcher angel in a position to exert some power or will over humans. This introduces a new idea about Satan into the picture. Satan is not only the chief of "fallen angels" who are evil, but also has the power to influence people. In other words, Satan can cause a person to do something evil.

In II Enoch, Satan is chief of the angels who gets power-hungry and so is cast out of heaven to become chief of demons. This story is the origin of the notion that Satan's pride caused him to be thrown out:

> *And I (God) gave orders that each (angel) should stand*
> *in his own rank. But one from the order of archangels*

*deviated, together with the division that was under his
authority. He thought up the impossible idea, that he
might place his throne higher than the clouds which are
above the earth, and that he might become equal to my
power. And I hurled him out from the height, together
with his angels*
——*II Enoch 29:4 (Old Testament Pseudepigrapha)*

When this story became popular during the Middle Ages as a
way to explain how evil came into the world, the idea of Satan as
a fallen angel was "read into" other texts. Old Testament stories
about Satan began to be re-interpreted from the perspective of this
"fallen angel" view of Satan. Think of the way, following the anti-
communist speeches of Senator Joseph McCarthy in the 1950's, the
U.S. went into a kind of hysteria described as a "red scare." All of
a sudden, previously harmless, off-hand remarks were reinterpreted
as endorsing communism. Actors and actresses were blacklisted
and kept from work. People began to see "evil communists"
threatening national security.

The same phenomenon was at work in the story of Satan as the
chief of the demons and a fallen angel. The serpent in Genesis 3
came to be perceived as an incarnation of Satan. Other Old
Testament writings such as Ezekiel 28: 14-19 were read through the
lens of the story of Satan as a fallen angel. The staying power of
this story comes from its incorporation in folklore and art.

### Conclusions About Satan In the Bible

Is there a "Biblical view" of Satan? The answer to this question
is both yes and no. Both Jewish and Christian scriptures talk about
the Devil, Satan, or Demons in a variety of places. But strictly
speaking, there is no single, uniform view of Satan in the Bible.

Instead we can speak about a plurality of Biblical perspectives on the problem of evil and on Satan, perspectives that developed and changed over time in response to changing understandings about God and the human condition. Rather than a Biblical view, there exist multiple understandings of Satan in the Bible.

In our time, the dialogue continues in the face of such huge experiences of destruction as the Holocaust of the Jewish people, the threat of nuclear destruction, and the South African experience of Apartheid. As was true in generations before us, we too draw from many sources including scripture, art, literature, philosophy, and science in our efforts to answer difficult questions about the nature of evil and suffering.

### Adolescent Satanism, the Bible, and Religious Tradition

Adolescent Satan worship bears little relationship to any particular Biblical tradition about Satan. In their beliefs about Satan, however, teens involved in Satan worship utilize a variety of understandings, some of which are informed by one or another Biblical perspectives. These young people commonly describe Satan as the chief of the forces of evil, or the "Prince of Death." Sometimes the "Prince of Death" title relates to Satan as the opposite of Christ who sometimes is called the "Prince of Peace."

### Other Sources for Contemporary Views of Satan

Two twelve-year-old girls were describing a movie they saw together that afternoon. In animated voices and with graphic detail they recounted the plot of the movie, which involved some unseen and evil force that moved through a small town and "took over the people." "One by one they all went crazy and then they would just end up being found dead in their beds with this sick smile on their faces, and a piece of paper with the word 'Satan' in blood always showed up near the bed. Some had their hearts ripped out, too." When asked about their perspectives on the Devil, not surprisingly these two girls described "a scary force that works in the dark to get people", and "He makes you promise your soul to him by signing in blood." These young teens also offered assurances that "it's true because we saw it in the movies."

Teens are major consumers of the many films and books classified as "horror stories." The images from these sources provide teens with a wealth of imaginative material for their views of Satan. Many of these films incorporate stories of sacrifice, rape, enslavement of women, and murder of infants. *Indiana Jones and the Temple of Doom*, while not on the subject of satanism, depicts an underground cult where people have their hearts ripped out of their bodies. These are the kinds of images that are common today in films and on TV which help form a young person's sense of "personified evil"—that which is scary or the demonic.

Another important source for adolescent views of Satan come from lyrics. Music is so central in the lives of teens. Liking a particular style, group, or musical performer helps establish identity. Teens express a part of who they are in the type of music they listen to. It helps to differentiate them from their parents and other adults. Music also provides an almost automatic connection to peers who share similar musical taste. Music becomes a sort of "instant shared history" between two young people who may have just met but know all the lyrics to a particular group's music and attend all their concerts.

The music industry counts on the teen market to keep buying recordings—and is willing to manipulate a time-honored truth to increase its sales: "if the parents hate it or forbid it, the teenagers will love it." And so a generation of young people bought record albums picturing Elvis Presley in mid-gyration on their covers, much to the chagrin and outrage of parents. Those images soon were replaced by "spacey" looking pictures of long haired male singing groups with names like "Strawberry Alarm Clock" and "The Beatles." Again, young people purchased these recordings sometimes over the protests of their parents.

It is difficult for teens today to find something with equal shock value. Sexually explicit movements and long hair on men now comprise the daily fare of television and hardly call for much comment. These days we seem to require a special brand of violence or strangeness to capture our attention. Some people are finding these elements in the lyrics, photographs and concert images of performers of "heavy metal" music.

In a song entitled "Altar of Sacrifice" by the group Slayer, the lyrics paint an image of Satan as one for whom a "high priest" (presumably male) murders a "pure virgin" (presumably female). It is a portrait of extreme male power over a helpless woman, with Satan portrayed as the one who requires or "commands" it. The high priest wields the power of death, and yet death is Satan's responsibility. Many such lyrics suggest themes of domination and violence mixed with sex, all in the service of Satan.

Some lyrics go so far as to offer what Ann Rodgers-Melnick calls "a vague theology of suicide."

A song entitled "Holy Hell" by the group Possessed extends Satan's image from "one who is connected to death" to "Satan means dying." And Satan is portrayed as the one who gives both death and new life. The further suggestion in these lyrics is that there is something "bonding" about "going to Satan's land," the land of death. One thing is certain: in a country where teen suicide rates are frighteningly ascending, the creators and marketers of such music definitely manage to get our attention. Such musical recordings also get the attention of adolescents and provide them with yet another source for their imaginative portraits of Satan.

## There's Always the Newspaper

Another often underestimated source for perspectives about Satan comes from the daily news. There, one can find headlines such as this one from the January 16, 1989 edition of the *Philadelphia Inquirer*: "Allegations of Satanism Shock Town." Or, in the *Sunday News Journal* of Wilmington, Delaware, on October 15, 1989 this headline greeted readers: "Police Fear Animal Abuse Work of Devil Cult." A quick scan of the newspapers of major cities reveals that satanism is being held responsible for everything from the murder or disappearance of children to the famous McMartin Preschool trials to causing the San Francisco Giants football team to have a poor season! Most of the images of Satan from such reports suggest a violent, powerful, child-harming agent who has the ability to directly influence world events.

## Images from Inner Depths:
## The Unconscious as a Source

Some researchers believe that an important but often unconsidered source of adolescent devil imagery comes from basic archetypal images of the "bad father"—images carried deep within the psyche of all human beings. Others suggest that devil images come out of the pre-verbal experiences of infancy when a baby undergoes an experience of abandonment by either parent. But the child can ill afford to hate the parent upon whom she or he depends so completely. So the child performs a defensive function of splitting off the internal image of the "bad parent" into a separate entity, thereby preserving the relationship with the "good parent". Some researchers contend that this split off image of the "bad parent" forms the clay from which images of the devil are shaped.

Some adolescent concepts of Satan certainly involve the use of polarized supernatural or cosmic metaphors which lend themselves well to this splitting mechanism[7]:  good vs. evil, God vs. Satan, light vs. dark, weakness vs. power.  Peter Olsson's description of the unconscious as a source for satanic imagery contends that satanism offers youth "supernatural father figures" through which teens attempt to compensate for "a physically or psychologically absent father of their childhoods."[8] These theorists are saying that negative experiences of fathers, or abandonment by fathers, provides the psychological,  unconscious "stuff" out of which images of Satan arise!  Adolescents then unconsciously use satanism as an attempt to recapitulate (re-do with a different, more favorable outcome) the father-child relationship.

### A Patchwork Quilt of Sources for the Image of Satan

Adolescent satanism emerges in American culture where virtually everyone can identify the character of Satan but with little agreement about the meaning of that character.  Similarly, there also exists a plurality of sources for who or what an adolescent perceives Satan to be.  Some of these sources are common, shared aspects of life in America:  film and news images.  Others are specific to a particular religious heritage.  Some of the sources are not even directly about Satan, but are part of the composite well of pictures available to the imagination, associated with that which is frightening, unknown, powerful or evil.  All of these and more become part of the composite portrait of meaning intended by adolescents who identify themselves with satanism.

# Chapter 6

## WHEN HELP IS NEEDED

A story in the newspaper begins with the headline: "Allegations of Satanism Shock Town." The story goes on to tell of a small town police sergeant who watches a television program on satanism and then begins connecting overturned tombstones, graffiti and other incidents to the practice of satanism. Then the same town is shocked by the suicide of a young man surrounded with satanic symbolism and tapes of heavy metal music groups. People in the town wonder  why they never saw any signs of satanism before and how the death of this young man might have been prevented.

A parent, seeing strange doodling that might be satanic symbols on his teenage son's notebooks, wonders if his son's withdrawal, isolation, and general avoidance of the family is "normal adolescence" or if he should be worried. "I saw an article about kids who worship the devil and that started me thinking, 'Is that what Steve is getting into?'  And what do I do if it is?' "

A teacher observes three of her students change their friends, manner of dress, and attitude in class. "They wear black all the time. Well, that's not so strange, because all of these kids do that. But they dyed every part of their hair—even eyebrows—deep black, and started showing up late for class with tattoos of upside down crosses on their arms, things like that. These kids were friends before, but they also hung around with some other people. Now they keep to themselves, whisper a lot, and sometimes they seem, well, out of it. I think they might be using drugs. And I think they're in a cult of some kind—maybe satanic. What should I do?"

Given the understanding about the nature of adolescent satanism as an experience likened with the developmental processes of teens, there are some important ways for adults to reach out and offer help. There also exist some dangers or pitfalls that can happen when well-intentioned, caring people try to offer help.

## The Danger of Overreacting

Everywhere adults who care about teenagers are expressing concern about how to recognize satanism, and what to do about it when they see it. Many adults, suspicious about sensational reports of satanic sacrifice of animals in the local park, want to avoid giving too much attention or credence to behavior that might be linked to adolescent satanism. "I don't want to reinforce to a kid that they can get my attention by acting weird," one counselor remarked. "But I also want to help them if they need it. I don't know much about religion so I'm probably not the best person to deal with satanic kids anyway. Funny, though, it still gets me upset when they say nasty things about religion and God."

This counselor's desire *not* to reward inappropriate or provocative behavior with undue attention suggests an important awareness on her part: the realization that adults can be easily "hooked" into overreacting by teens displaying behaviors, clothing, music, and symbols linked to satanism. The tendency to react strongly originates from a positive source: care and concern for the young person, and the desire to be helpful. One way to understand overreaction is to view it as an excess of response. Instead of simply responding to the situation at hand, a person responds excessively, or overreacts. That person is responding to something beyond just the specifics of the situation at hand.

## Overreaction as Too Much of a Good Thing

Overreaction occurs when a person attempts to respond to a situation of concern to them, but the response is fueled in part by strong emotional energies to which the responder is blind. For example, a woman in an office where a few of the other workers took extended breaks and left work early one day became aware that she was speaking in an exceedingly sharp tone to her friend and co-worker. The co-worker had done nothing unusual. But when he got up from his desk for a break and invited her to come along, she sarcastically said, "no thanks, somebody around here has to work." Then she stormed away. When her co-worker later asked about her strong reaction to his innocent invitation, she could speak openly about her discomfort at the work habits of others in the office. Yet her response still seemed out of proportion to the situation. Upon further reflection, the woman realized that she resented working long hours in the office and then going home to household and child care responsibilities while her husband "took an extended break" when he came home for the evening. This woman's response to her co-worker was an overreaction. It was fueled by emotional energy from her marriage, emotions she did not even realize were so strong.

We are in the greatest danger of overreacting whenever the situation contains elements of something really important to us. That makes adolescent satanism fertile territory for overreaction. Adolescent satanism touches on elements as huge and significant as one's beliefs and convictions about the transcendent universe—

the nature of the human soul, ideas about afterlife, questions about supernatural and cosmic forces. It addresses concerns as personal as one's beliefs about appropriate norms for sexual intimacy. It pokes fun at religious perspectives and faith convictions in ways that can needle even those who profess a cool detachment toward organized religion. That's because adolescent satanism can bring to the foreground questions about what one believes about God.

Adults encounter adolescent satanism most frequently in the form of a rebellious, acting-out teenager who does not respond to adult concern or authority. Feelings of being incapable or incompetent can also be a source of overreaction.

Overreaction can also come from the positive desire on the part of parents and youth professionals not to abandon young people by "being in denial" about the depth or significance of their troubles. Many teens in treatment testify to the way adults acted blindly to their chemical use or behavioral cries for help until something drastic (legal trouble or a failed suicide attempt) forced those adults to take notice. Responding excessively to young people is likely to result from guilt or fear about responding insufficiently.

The main problem with overreaction is that instead of being helpful, it plays directly into the power game of the satanically involved teen. When adults identify the primary significance of adolescent satanism as religious, and paint the issues in terms of a cosmology of Good and Evil battling over the world of that young person, then adolescent satanism takes on huge power. Cosmic significance has been accorded it. Attributing too much significance to satanism heightens the sense of power that young people attain from their expression of it. If adults react strongly at the first sign of an occult-oriented book, teens get the message that such interests have real power to get adults upset, or at least to capture their attention.

## A Helpful Alternative: Planned Response

How can a person avoid overreaction when faced with the evidence or possibility of a young person's satanic involvement? And what are more helpful ways of responding? One way to avoid overreaction is to think through the issues and perspectives surrounding adolescent satanism *before* dealing with it. The goal of such a process is self-education about satanism, and also education about the self. The question, "What buttons of mine are likely to get pushed by this?" becomes very helpful when answered ahead of time. The table below suggests some questions to reflect upon. They will help you plan your response to adolescent satanism.

1. What do I believe now about Satan? About evil? How have my beliefs changed over time?
2. What are my beliefs about a Higher Power or God? How have these beliefs changed since my childhood? If someone wanted to offend me based on my beliefs, what would be the best way for them to do so?
3. How do I feel when someone close to me has different beliefs? How do I want to feel? How do I really feel? How do I feel if someone challenges my ideas?
4. What was my life like as a fourteen-year-old? A sixteen-year-old? What were the biggest problems I had then? What was good for me about being a teenager?
5. How do I respond when a teenager starts to argue with me? Acts bored with me or ignores me? How did my parents respond when I was a teen and

I argued/acted bored/ignored them? If a teenager really wanted to bring to the surface my feelings of inadequacy about being a good parent/teacher/counselor, what should he or she do?

6. How do I feel about the values expressed in satanic ritual and ideology? What are some of my own values about how to treat other people or animals?

By reflecting on one's own ideas and experiences, especially one's own adolescence, and identifying some of the "buttons that may get pushed" by satanic-involved teens, the danger of overreaction can be minimized. Then adults are free to respond, aware of their own feelings and issues, but not driven into overreaction by them.

## The Danger of Minimizing

A second danger some adults may experience in the effort to respond to adolescent satanism is on the opposite pole of overreaction: underreaction, or minimizing teen satanism. Minimizing a response to adolescent satanism happens when adults either avoid seeing the patterns of behavior that suggest that a young person is in trouble, or fail to give any significance to what they observe. A parent decided not to respond when she began to see satanic symbols in her son's room, and made light of his inclusion of those symbols on his clothing. When her son began to isolate himself, she remembered reading that such behavior was characteristic of teens, and did not attribute any special significance to his withdrawal from the family. She noticed his changing musical tastes and peer group and remembered similar changes she had experienced as an adolescent. When her son was arrested a few months later for vandalizing church property by spray-painting vulgar language on the walls and breaking into the sanctuary area (he and his friends were looking for consecrated hosts to use in their ritual), the parent was surprised when police associated his actions with satanism.

Minimizing may be as simple as failing to notice patterns of change that indicate some kind of trouble for the young person. It may come from a fear of overreaction or "coming on too strong." It may be an honest and unintended failure to put together the available clues. Minimizing can also happen as the result of "over-understanding" teens.

Is it really possible to understand someone too much? When understanding ("that's typical of teenagers") allows adults to rationalize or explain away serious problems and behaviors, then over-understanding is occurring. When over-understanding leads to an increased tolerance for unacceptable or dysfunctional behaviors from teens, adults are at risk of responding to adolescent satanism through minimizing.

### A Helpful Alternative: Attending to Patterns

The seriousness and significance of adolescent satanism cannot be measured with any single indicator. Finding a *Satanic Bible* in a young person's room does not necessarily indicate a problem. A young person who expresses a preference for heavy metal music is not necessarily involved in satanism. Instead of looking for individual indicators, it is helpful to watch for the emergence of patterns, preoccupations, and duration of interest in things associated with Satanism.

The next section offers a list of common features that may signal some level of involvement in satanism by a teenager. Attending to patterns means watching for the occurrence of several of these features. It means watching for increases in intensity or duration of interest. What makes any one of these items suggestive of a problem depends on how it is being used by the teen. Is there evidence of unhealthy preoccupation or a dysfunctional coping style emerging in the young person's behaviors? Are more than one of these features visible? The items with an asterisk differ in that their occurrence should always be treated as a sign of concern requiring professional help.

### Some Typical Signs of Adolescent Satanism

• *Display of satanic symbols and/or evidence of rituals*—A variety of symbols, including the goats head, upside down cross, pentagrams, black candles, various names of Satan, or the number 666, have come to be associated with satanism. At issue for assigning the significance of symbols is whether their use is a "passing fad" that disappears as interest wanes, or whether such symbols proliferate and increase over a period of time. Do they appear with other features in this list? The use of satanic symbols alone may not be a problem, but in connection with other indicators, suggests a pattern of concern.

• *Preoccupation with heavy metal music containing satanic lyrics*—Does this behavior reflect a dramatic change for the young person? Has she/he shifted completely from a previously enjoyed musical style? Does she/he utilize the lyrics beyond simply listening to them, e.g., as an encouragement to act in a self-destructive manner? For many teens this music either lacks interest or does not cause problems. While its existence as part of the music world of teens shows no particularly redeeming or valuable qualities, and may even contribute to the problems associated with teen satanism, it is tempting to scapegoat this (or other rock music) as being the problem. The issue is how a particular teenager uses this music.

• *Self-mutilation and other self-destructive behavior*\*—Are there signs that the young person is carving symbols into her/his skin or cutting her/himself? Does the teen act in unsafe and potentially harmful ways with weapons? Is there a preoccupation with talking and writing about death?

• *Drug abuse*\*—Does the teen show mood swings? Is he/she spending time with known drug users? Have grades dropped or changed? Is there "physical evidence" of chemical use such as paraphernalia, odors, unexplained instances of money or valuables missing? Is there a noticeable change in affect, seen either as a loss of energy/depression, or in unusual hyperactivity? The link between satanism and drug abuse is strong. Some experts also note a third point of linkage—satanism, drug abuse, and gang involvement.

• *Changes in peer group, cothing, and activities*—A young person's change to a new friendship group may signal a difficulty, particularly if the new peer group is radically different than the young person's former peers. What does this group like to do together? Are they usually secretive about their activities? Has the teen dropped out of activities that formerly were at a high level of importance to her/him, such as sports or music? What replaces these activities in the young person's schedule? Given the range of expected experimentation with styles of dress during adolescence, is the teen making radical changes that incorporate satanic symbolism?

• *Violence and destructive behavior toward persons, animals, or property*\*—When an adolescent becomes violent, it is essential to get help quickly to deal with the violence and its underlying origins. Satanically linked violence often takes the form of the capture, killing and/or mutilation of animals including pets for their blood; threats or actual use of physical force against people; sexual abuse and exploitation as a part of satanic ritual; and violent destruction of property, particularly the desecration of grave sites and churches.

•*An absorbing preoccupation with the occult*—While interest in occult matters occurs naturally during adolescence, satanically-involved teens display an intense preoccupation with occult books and films to the detriment of other subjects and interests. Their interest lasts over a considerable time period as well. Is the young person merely investigating one interest among several in their reading, or are they memorizing sections of *The Satanic Bible?* Does the teen seem to be acting on the basis of their interest in some way? How is this interest affecting their overall attitude and well-being?

•*Manifesting signs of sexual abuse victimization*\*—Young women are particularly at risk to be victimized as a part of their participation in adolescent satanism, but men are also victims of sexual abuse. Common signs include exceptionally poor hygiene and self-care, eating disorders, withdrawal, sexually provocative or suggestive behaviors that are inappropriate, chemical use to deal with feelings from trauma, patterns of abusive relationships, depression, sleep disturbances. Some people show an aversion and avoidance of the abuser(s), while others become protective of them. As is the case with satanism, sexual abuse cannot be determined on the basis of a single clue, and many of these signs may indicate other issues unrelated to abuse. If there is any reason to suspect sexual abuse, getting the help of a counselor or therapist trained to deal with abuse is imperative.

The above section gives some of the more common warning signs of adolescent involvement in satanism. But because teen satanic involvement has different degrees and meanings, adults must attend to how these various features are manifested in the life of a particular teen, and how they appear to effect that teen.

## The Danger of Oversimplification

A third response of some adults to adolescent satanism involves oversimplifying the young person's experience. Oversimplification means yielding to the temptation to compartmentalize or "box away" what has occurred for a teen involved in satanic activities. It occurs from the natural and positive efforts to make manageable that which exceeds easy explanation. Because satanism concerns an encounter with what has sometimes been named supernatural or transcendent, it is natural to seek ways to "manage" the complexity of satanism. If an adolescent participates in satanic ritual—even a ritual that happens on the spur of the moment, which the group makes up as they go along—the fact that the setting for these activities is satanic affects the meaning in the minds of the young people engaged in them.

It is common to find teens in chemical dependency treatment who have a history of satanic involvement during the period they used chemicals. They may articulate how their satanic activities met needs, and even the power dimension of satanism—how it worked to make them feel more powerful. But those same teens will frequently "get stuck" over feelings that they have given themselves to Satan, and can never return to being loved by a Higher Power/God. For them there remains some aspect of meaning that involved encounter with mystery, the supernatural, and the spiritual realms. Many teens express profound fear that they "can't go back to God." Others whose concern finds expression in less explicitly religious language will express fears about "never really getting out of the dark."

Oversimplification is an effort to explain away aspects of satanic involvement as being beyond physical reality. It represents a tendency to deny the depth-level significance of what teens experience, a dismissal of the spiritual aspects of satanism for teens. In spite of the fact that adolescent satanism is not a religious or faith attachment to Satan, despite the reality that adolescent satanism is not essentially about faith, there are spiritual implications of the experience for youths. It has an impact on their spirituality.

Another form of oversimplification happens when adults show a desire to deal with the non-material, spiritual qualities *only*, and do not address underlying needs of a satanically involved teen. "I see the whole thing as spiritual," said one parent in a school meeting. "If our kids weren't living in a spiritual vacuum, then Satan worship would disappear." Other parents at the meeting suggested that, in addition to the spiritual aspects of satanism for youth, there were other problems such as chemical use, sexuality, or anti-authority issues. "Those are important problems," she replied, "but we have to get at the real problem. These kids have no religion." Unfortunately, the "real" problem is rarely so simple. It instead contains multiple dimensions and facets which need to be addressed together, holistically, with the young person.

## A Helpful Response: Listening and Linking

The unique and personal quality of individual perceptions of the spiritual world presents both a challenge and an opportunity for adults who care about satanic youth. The opportunity is to enter the world of an adolescent through the eyes of their experience, to walk with them and listen in order to understand how they view a situation. The challenge comes in the need to both accept that young person's perceptions of what happened, and to call them to new possibilities for understanding it—new perspectives to which they do not have access on their own. No one can say with truth to another person, "You did not really have that experience the way you described it." Similarly, if teens attach metaphysical or supernatural meaning to their experiences with satanism, little is gained if adults attempt to invalidate that experience as "unreal." What can be offered, however, is a link between what the young person describes and what additional perspectives might be brought to the situation.

Kevin described his participation in satanic ritual as "coming face to face with the spirit world." His belief—that he was compelled to conduct a ritual by the spirits of the dead who are trying to get Kevin to join them—leaves him with a feeling of fear that he is being "pursued" by evil spirits. Kevin has no doubt about the personal quality of these spirits. "It's kinda creepy to me now, but there are some dead people who want me." And yet, in treatment he was invited by the team of counselors, chaplains, and occupational therapists who worked with him to consider the way his depression and response to the deaths of two close friends made Kevin the one who "wanted some dead people." Kevin eventually began to address the way his satanic activities functioned as an effort to cope with an experience of loss he could neither understand nor accept.

Sometimes, though, listening is not an option. Many young people with an active satanic involvement refuse to talk about their ideas, beliefs, or experiences. In those situations, adults can take steps to assess the situation based on the evidence they observe. They can listen with their eyes and intuitions instead of only with their ears to understand what is going on in the world of the teen.

### What Are My Options?

Depending on the context in which an adult encounters teens (at home as a parent, at school as teacher, principal or counselor, in a treatment program) a variety of helpful resources are at hand to deal with adolescent satanism and its related issues. Community resources include: chemical health workers in the school; adolescent chemical dependency treatment programs; professional counselors and therapists experienced with adolescents; pastoral counselors, chaplains, and clergy with psychological training; mental health professionals including psychiatrists; and sexual abuse services. Planning a response can help. Adults concerned about teens can talk with professional and community resource persons and develop a referral list before the need to seek services arises. This way, they can find out who is best equipped to deal with teen satanism.

## Prevention-Oriented Responses

A recent study by the Search Institute, a Minneapolis-based research group concerned with adolescents, looks at the issue of "at-risk" teens in terms of the many "indicators" of behaviors that put teens in danger of serious trouble. The findings of this study indicate certain factors promoting positive development of youth, and conclude that "with one important exception (the provision of economic security), most of these factors can be altered in an individual young person's surroundings if the adults in that young person's family and community consider it important enough to do so." The study goes on to name sixteen "external assets," features present in the family or community that mediate against a young person getting into trouble. "The more assets a given teenager reports being present in his or her life, the fewer the at-risk behaviors that teenager displays."[1]

Some of these assets help create a network of support and valuing of the adolescent. These include: (1) family support, (2) parent (s) as a social resource for the teen (someone they can go to for advice and encouragement), (3) parent communication, with frequent and in-depth conversations reported by the adolescents in the study, (4) parent involvement in schooling, (5) communication with other adults, (6) the availability of non-parent adults that the young person knows and can turn to as resources, and (7) a positive school climate.

Other external assets identified in the Search Institute study have to do with setting limits or controls on behavior. These features include: (1) parental standards that allow teens to know what parents expect of them, and know the consequences of inappropriate behavior: (2) parental disciplining that means teens are held accountable for their behavior, (3) parental monitoring, by which parents expect to know the activities and location of their teens, (4) time at home, and (5) positive peer influence.

The final category of external assets addressed in the study concerns what the Search Institute calls the structured use of time: (1) involved in music, spending some time each week in lessons or practice, (2) involved in school extracurricular activities, (3) involved in community organizations or activities, (4) involved in church or synagogue activities.

These findings support the earlier discussion about the coping abilities of teens because they suggest that during adolescence—a time when certain internal strengths may actually diminish— it is possible to prevent a teen's movement into the "at-risk" group by adding appropriate external supports before problems occur.

## Some Treatment Responses to Adolescent Satanism

The close correlation between chemical use and satanic activity by adolescents means that treatment programs will see more than their fair share of young people identifying themselves as satanic. Likewise, the self-destructive aspects of participation in satanism means that adolescent mental health workers will also be faced with young people reporting or manifesting some level of involvement. While many of the responses discussed above fit several situations, there are some responses that are specific to treatment and recovery.

### Chemical Dependency, Recovery, and Satanism

Recovery is a process involving complex and multiples changes for a young person. Spirituality— and spiritual recovery— lies at the heart of recovery from chemical dependency. Spirituality concerns a person's way of life and our way of being in the world. It involves bumping up against those realities that include and reach beyond the boundaries of the personal and interpersonal exchanges. It is the encounter and awareness of realities as intangible as love and as ineffable as the knowledge that there exists "something bigger than me" at work. Spirituality has to do with a basic sense of self-acceptance, warts and all. It includes the ability to deal with the limits of human existence—unmet hopes and desires, failed expectations, inability to live up to an ideal. It is about a sense of balance in life, balance between the self's power and ability to influence the world, and the relative lack of power humans have over the various happenings of life. Spirituality concerns the meaning a person ascribes to all these features of existence. The final chapter of this book will explore these ideas further by taking a look at healthy adolescent spirituality.

Many of the issues involved with adolescent satanism relate directly to issues of chemical dependency. What are some helpful treatment responses for dealing with satanism?

### Unmasking the Power Pact

Adolescents in treatment who are addressing issues of power— their lack of power over chemicals and their efforts to have some power in the family—need help and encouragement to look at the power dimensions of their satanic involvement. "I liked the feeling of being important at school. I know I could scare people. It felt powerful." Such frank acknowledgment by teens of the central role of power in their attraction to satanism helps them look honestly at their past behaviors and deal with the real issues, instead of "getting stuck" on the external or overt characteristics of satanism such as beliefs about the Devil. Dealing with the various aspects of how satanism and power are linked for teens—power and peers, parents, the self, and the supernatural provides adolescents in treatment with some entry points into other underlying issues by giving them a new frame of reference for understanding their own satanic involvement. It is much easier for most teens to acknowledge their efforts to achieve some power over their parents by scaring the parents with occult imagery, than it is for those same teens to deal with their feelings of guilt about injuring an animal, hurting their parents, or even "committing an unforgiveable sin" against God.

### Naming for the Self the Attractions of Satanism

Counselors and other members of the care team can help a young person who has made an initial decision for recovery to think through and identify what makes satanism attractive to them. "I like it because you get to make your own rules." "It's about being part of the group doing rituals." I feel cool when I'm with those people." Based on these types of statements, some adolescents are capable of identifying how satanism met needs for them. Many teens, for whom insight-oriented therapy is appropriate, can begin to see the attractions of satanism in terms of the underlying issues such as identity belonging, sexuality, authority, and spirituality. These teens find help in "re-framing" their understanding about their participation in satanic activity. They move away from judgmental or blaming language to a new perspective, seeing their satanic involvement as a way to deal with unmet needs and cope with difficulties.

Other teens, with whom a more behavioral approach is warranted, can begin to address whether the various behaviors associated with their particular expression of satanism actually achieve the desired goal, and consider the consequences of those behaviors. They can also practice alternative behaviors. A teen who lacks well-developed insight skills may not grasp that they use acting out behaviors tied to satanism as a way to get adult attention. But that teen can begin to look at how parents and teachers distance themselves from him or her in response to verbal abuse and can then practice some behaviors that yield different results.

### Breaking Up Is Hard To Do

Frequently, young people are reluctant to let go of satanism, even after doing considerable treatment work and making progress toward recovery. "Why can't Satan be my Higher Power?" is the question raised by many teens in Twelve Step programs. How can treatment professionals help teens who seem intent on maintaining an identification with satanism? First, it is more helpful to "go with the resistance" of the teen instead of getting into power struggles. Give them exercises to prove how Satan as a Higher Power will support their recovery. Such a paradoxical approach may initially appear to give increased energy to the whole issue of satanism. But quickly the young person will need to address whether their identification with satanism supports sobriety or chemical use.

Second, adolescents in treatment need help to see the connections between their drug use and satanism, just as they need help to make connections between their drug use and failing grades or conflicted family relationship. It is common during the evaluation or early phases of treatment to hear a young person say, "Sure I flunked algebra. But that has nothing to do with my chemical use. I just don't like math." Similarly, many youths initially avoid connecting their satanic activities with drug use.

Third, in Twelve Step programs that call for the recovering person to acknowledge some reality called "Higher Power" adolescents can be re-directed to deal with the Second and Third Steps as steps fundamentally concerned with a *positive* Higher Power who can support their recovery. At this point, many adolescents come forth with assertions about what they do *not* believe, and how their ideas about God or Higher Power are different from the concepts of the Twelve Steps. Some of the energy is healthy separation from others—an effort to claim some ability/authority for self-determination of beliefs. Many persons, adolescents and adults alike, find in the open spirituality of the Twelve Steps a liberation from past concepts of God or spirituality that have been oppressive.

This struggle—to move from what one does *not* affirm or does not believe, toward some initial affirmations of what can be trusted—comprises one of the most critically important struggles in treatment. For young people with a history of satanic involvement, the struggle may be complicated by fears of rejection by the God they once rejected.

Or the struggle to affirm a Higher Power may take place in an "experiential vacuum" if a teen has never had a trusting relationship. The young person who never has had a relationship of care and trust, who lacked those nurturing relationships of infancy that set the stage for the later ability to establish a bond of trust with another, has few resources to draw upon toward imagining something as abstract as a Higher Power. Satanism becomes easy for such persons because it requires no foundation of trust, no attachments of the heart. The move away from satanism for such an adolescent will not come easily. Such a young person will need to be offered something very concrete with which to replace the satanism they resist releasing. A positive, trusting experience with a primary care provider in treatment or with the treatment peer group may be just the necessary first step.

### Shame On Who?

Sometimes adolescents in recovery carry a heavy load of guilt or shame about their past involvement in satanic ritual. Often guilt or remorse is the feeling expressed when they look at the specific behaviors associated with satanism.     Guilt comes from the recognition that the behavior harms another, or breaks the teens' own values.

"I feel guilty because I made my little sister promise not to tell mom that I was leaving the house to be with my friends. She knew I was into devil stuff, which scared her a lot. She's just a little kid. But I told her that the Devil would come and get her if she ever said anything. Now I look back, and I think, 'How could I do that to her?' It must have been awful for her, but I didn't care then. I just wanted to do what I wanted to do." The young man making these comments had become painfully aware of the affect of his actions on someone he loves. At the point when he could no longer deny the hurtful impact of his actions on his sister, he felt guilty.

Not far removed from guilt is the feeling of shame. Shame is the feeling that results from the young person's belief that they somehow are broken or "bad." It is not simply a matter of "bad behaviors," but a deep and wrenching feeling that the behaviors happened because of a fundamental flaw in the person. Fifteen-year-old Kara, who has a history of oppositional and aggressive behavior, looked back upon her participation in a ritual in which she and a peer cut a satanic symbol into the thigh of a dog. "Now I ask, 'what sort of person would do something so cruel? We put a belt around his mouth so he wouldn't bite us, but his eyes were terrified. I can't believe that I did such a horrible thing. I was high. But I didn't have to do that. I feel like a really bad person, like there must be something major wrong with me. I'm so ashamed. And I don't want anybody to know about it, because I know what they'll think of me if they know I did that."

Teens who feel ashamed about their satanic behaviors work hard to avoid talking about what they have done for fear of being judged by others as harshly as they judge themselves. If these teens can understand their own actions as efforts to cope instead of as evidence that they are "bad", the shift can be quite freeing.

"I was doing the best I could do. With satan worship, I picked a way of dealing with my situation that hurt me and a lot of other people. I wish I hadn't done it that way, and it doesn't excuse what I did. But now I understand why I did what I did, and I know I'm not a bad person. Plus I'm working on those issues in my treatment now."

This insight came from Tony, an older adolescent who had difficulty forgiving himself for his satanic behaviors, which included hurting a neighbor's pet. His healing process involved his self-identified need to talk with a priest about vandalizing a Catholic church ("only somebody really bad would do what I did...I broke into a church and had sex in there"), and about destructive and violent acts against helpless animals over which he felt strong remorse. Being able to tell a person whom he accepted as a religious authority about his actions—and to receive the acceptance and support of that person—was a powerful experience of forgiveness for him. Teens need opportunities in treatment to address their guilt and to experience a sense of forgiveness appropriate to their particular faith tradition and emerging spirituality.

### When Help Is Needed: A Call for Balance

This chapter provides some clues to recognize the presence of satanism. It also addresses ways for adults to respond. Several of those responses may appear paradoxical, as with the concern to neither overreact nor minimize the significance of a particular teen's manifestation of satanism. This is a call for balance. It emerges out of my conviction that adults can respond to these young people in ways that both respect their experiences and call them to grow into a hopeful future.

# Chapter 7

## Toward a Healthy Adolescent Spirituality

*"I'm not too sure what I believe. That's ok, isn't it? I mean, a lot of my friends seem to know. But I'm searching. Actually I think I'll always be searching."*
—Sheri, seventeen years old

*"I was lying in bed, trying to sleep. This thought kept going through my head like songs from the radio do, even after you turn it off. I can't exactly put it into words, but it was something to do with knowing my life could matter a lot to somebody in this world. Who knows? I might just be in the right place at the right time to make a difference."*
—a sixteen-year-old male

*" . . . it's all in the music for me."*
—Tim, fourteen years old

*"When I'm with my friends and I know they really understand what I'm going through, and they support me, and I can do the same for them, that's what it's all about."*
—Karen, fifteen years old

What are some marks of healthy adolescent spirituality? Most of this book has been devoted to looking at what happens to teens when satanism becomes a dysfunctional way of dealing with developmental transitions and difficulties in coping. While adolescent satanism is a matter primarily related to development with religious and ritualistic overtones, this basically non-religious experience can have a huge impact on the spirituality of the adolescent. Its potential for affecting adolescent spirituality comes from its ability to touch so many aspects of a young person's life.

## Defining That Which Can Not Be Held

Spirituality is almost indefinable. Its nature resists definition. It cannot be held or placed in a container. In the previous chapter I named spirituality as a way of life, our way of being in the world. Another way of defining spirituality is to think of it as a person's process of relating to the self, to other, and to God/Higher Power. That is, spirituality involves a here-and-now, tangible experience of me-as-myself—a sense of individuality and autonomous self. This aspect of spirituality includes how persons feel about themselves, and how they adapt to challenges to the self. Spirituality also involves an experience of myself-with-others—a sense of community and relatedness. This aspect of spirituality includes how persons form significant attachments and cope with losses, as well as their relationships to the larger communities (such as family, neighborhood, and even the world community!). Spirituality also involves an awareness of that which is radically "not-me", a relationship between the self and that "partly mysterious/partly knowable" reality which exists beyond the boundaries of ordinary human interaction.

This transcendent aspect of spirituality is sometimes called God, Higher Power, the Holy, or even Ultimate Concern.

Spirituality refers to that aspect of life which finds us somehow "caught up" in this something-beyond-ourselves. Spiritual awareness involves our discovery that, being caught up by the "something more", we begin to live intentionally in relation to it, living out both a story and a lifelong, searching journey.

The relational character of this third aspect of spirituality permits me to use the terms "faith" and "spirituality" somewhat interchangeably. Recalling an earlier discussion in Chapter 2 about the nature of faith as "trust in another," or the activity of "setting one's heart" upon a transcendent center of value and power, it becomes apparent that the activity of *faith* is also what I am describing above as the activity of spirituality: living in light of a relationship with the self, others and a Higher Power.

Some people may bristle at the use of the word "faith," perhaps associating it with a particular content of belief to which one must ascribe, or a particular form of belief, as in "the Catholic faith" or "the Muslim faith." Faith is less a specific content than a process and quality of human experience around which the particular beliefs making up one's world view are shared. As Fowler puts it, "Faith is a verb." Faith concerns our activity and way of "being and committing." But perhaps most important for teens, "faith is always *relational*. There is always *another* in faith."[1]

## Faith as a Developmental Process

I alluded earlier to the developmental nature of faith in a discussion about how the faith of a forty-year-old is appropriately different from that of a four-year-old. Faith or spirituality, like other aspects of human experience, grows and changes through time. James W. Fowler's well-known work, *Stages of Faith*, identifies structural passages of faith through which persons move during their life cycle. As with other kinds of development—for example, motor coordination or sexual maturation—there is a range of "optimal" time to be in a particular stage. Similarly, with faith there exists developmentally appropriate ways in which persons experience and express meaning, value, and transcendence.

Such a perspective about faith can be fruitful in understanding and working with young people around their spiritual issues, and can be particularly helpful in dealing with teens who have a history of satanic involvement. I will spell out in some detail the first four stages of Fowler's model, which are the stages concerning child and adolescent faith development. Some of this discussion recalls elements of the earlier chapter on adolescent development. But the emphasis here falls specifically upon the development of faith, understanding what constitutes a healthy adolescent spirituality.

Fowler's model identifies six stages of faith and the approximate age at which persons optimally find themselves within a particular stage. The stages relate to each other by forming a sequential pattern through which human beings move in their experience of spiritual development across the life cycle. It is possible for faith development to be arrested or delayed, just as other types of development can be affected by internal constraints on growth. The first three stages relate to child and adolescent faith development, and the fourth involve the transitional time from adolescence to young adulthood. Stage 5 (Conjunctive) and stage 6 (Universalizing) will not be addressed here since they are "adult" stages.

## STAGE 1: Intuitive-Projective Faith

Intuitive-Projective Faith is the stage of early childhood (around ages 4-8), when fact and fantasy blend together and thinking is concrete. Children in the intuitive projective stage of faith imitate what they perceive to be the faith of their parents. If their parents pray before meals at the table, the children take that on as an expression of faith.

These children are unaware that anyone else might perceive reality differently than they do. The world is the world from *their* perspective. And so there is a kind of egocentrism about this stage, which children cannot move  beyond until they acquire some ability to recognize that other people may see things from a different point of view.  Intuitive-Projective stage children are strongly oriented toward stories told to them—stories that can express externally the fears they feel within, stories that capture their imaginative and still vague fantasies about how the world works. Trust is a primary faith issue for children in this stage. The faith of children in the intuitive-projective stage relates to the stories given to them by parents and other adults.

## STAGE 2: Mythic-Literal Faith

The Mythic-Literal Faith stage typifies the school age child (6-12 years old), who becomes capable of construing cause-and-effect relationships: $x$ happened because of $y$. Children in the mythic-literal faith stage also gain the ability to recognize that other people perceive experiences in their own ways.  Together these factors lead to a concern for fairness. A typical mythic-literal perspective views God as one who punishes bad people/behaviors and rewards good people/behaviors.  God is imaged or picured as someone with human characteristics.  This stage sees a continuation of the central role of stories.  But now the child is able to construct her/his own story, albeit in a very literal and concrete way, as a way to express meaning.  Rituals related to faith are used by children in the mythic-literal stage, but have a one-dimensional quality.

## STAGE 3: Synthetic-Conventional Faith

Synthetic-Conventional Faith occurs around the onset of adolescence (around 12 years of age) and lasts until late adolescence, as the young person develops the capacity of abstract thinking and an expanded ability to take on the perspectives of other people. The adolescent can imagine not only how another person might feel in a certain situation ("John must feel like crawling under the floor and dying!") but also can think abut how another person perceives her or him ("When I spilled my milk at the lunch table, I knew John thought I was a klutz."). There exists a powerful drive to belong to a peer group (conformity) offset somewhat by an equally significant drive to establish one's unique identity (autonomy). In the context of these developmental dynamics, faith takes on a highly relational, personal character. The spirituality of adolescence, their construction of values and identity, and understanding of transcendence, is strongly shaped by affiliation with and conformity to a group. Symbols and their meanings go largely unexamined, but are important in helping the young person both shape and express their identity and values.

### STAGE 4:  Individuative-Reflective Faith

The fourth stage in Fowler's schema, Individuative-Reflective Faith, comes in late adolescence or early adulthood (if at all). The transition from the previous synthetic-conventional stage to this stage happens when a person begins to reflect critically upon their own beliefs and values, and then attains some critical distance that gives a new perspective.

A helpful way to see the transition between these two stages is to look at how they each utilize symbols. In stage 3 a chalice used in a religious ceremony is sacred. Its ability to express meaning is tied to the physical chalice itself, and cannot be separated from it. In stage 4, the physical chalice is a separate thing from the "meaning" it represents to the person—God's love, or participation in a community. A second important change is that authority is increasingly less dependent upon others (even the internalized voices of others in the form of the question "What will they think of me?"), and more securely self-directed. Instead of an external or internalized "they," there is an increasing and stronger reliance on an internalized "I."

## A Bias Toward Growth

Fowler's faith stages are much more complex than I have indicated in this brief summary. He spends considerable time addressing what influences transition from one stage to the next, and offers extensive theological reflection. He has been criticized for creating a "hierarchy of faith stages" in which it appears that persons in later stages are "more spiritual" or somehow superior to those at earlier stages. [2]

We are quite glad that a baby is a baby, and consider the baby to be whole and complete. Yet we certainly hope that when that baby becomes a sixteen-year-old, she will have developed beyond her earlier infantile capacities. While no value judgement is placed upon one stage, growth toward one's potential is good. Spiritual growth is a desirable thing, and so helping young people to grow spiritually, to grow in their faith, is a valuable endeavor.

## Stages of Faith and Adolescent Satanism

How does the decision to approach the spirituality of adolescents as an active, developing capacity rather than as a static content of belief affect perceptions of healthy adolescent spirituality? First, it suggests that there are age-appropriate aspects of spirituality. A person in late adolescence who consistently displays features of stage 2 faith will appear "developmentally arrested," or stuck, spiritually, in the same way that we might speak of someone whose physical maturation is arrested. And even though adults cannot "make" a young person go through the transition from one stage to another, they can provide opportunities for young people to realize their full potential.

Adolescent satanism, with its use of a fairly narrow range of symbols which are construed quite literally, and simplistic resolution of difficult questions poses a risk to adolescent spiritual growth. It is a risk that is also found in rigid and narrow religious theologies. Adolescent satanism traps teenagers in the early mythic-literal stage of faith. It can lock them into the mythic-literal stage where reality exists as a polarity between good and evil; where there are no grey areas or ambiguities; where symbols literally correspond to the thing they stand for; where the real and the make-believe may be difficult to distinguish; and where the determining principle for ethical action/justice is a kind of "eye for an eye" reciprocity. Adolescent satanism's emphasis on revenge against those who cause pain or difficulty is a "you hurt me, so now I'll hurt you" style of morality. It blurs the lines between fantasy and reality, with its notions of magic and spell-casting to manipulate events.

There is nothing inherently "wrong" with being in the mythic-literal stage of faith—especially if one is an eight-year-old! But when adolescents are locked into mythic-literal ways of being spiritual, and when their corresponding moral or ethical capacities are so limited, something is wrong. Healthy spirituality is a spiritual development that is appropriate to the age and age-related capacities of the person.

A developmental understanding of adolescent spirituality implies a certain fit between the issues of cognitive and moral development and those of faith development. A young person who has acquired the capacity for abstract thought, also acquires new possibilities for imagining a freer, less concrete concept of

God. The various aspects of development enhance one another. But this also suggests that they have the potential to limit one another. A person who never achieves much ability to think beyond concrete thought experiences a limited understanding of what God is like. It is interesting to speculate about whether stunted spiritual growth might also limit a person's capacities for psychosocial and mental development. If that is the case, then young people who are not encouraged and assisted to grow spiritually face other sorts of developmental interruptions. If adults who care for young people support their spiritual development, the young people's total growth and development as persons will be enhanced.

### What Does Healthy Adolescent Spirituality Look Like?

I recently saw a wonderful example of healthy teen spirituality. A large group of young people with whom I worked for the weekend gathered in a conference center in Kansas City. They came from places like Topeka and St. Louis, and from little towns named Liberal and Independence. Not many of them knew each other. But with the help of their adult leaders who structured some experiences for them and allowed for unstructured time too, this unrelated band of teenagers entered into relationship with one another. They became a community.

It was a very physical weekend—this group was comfortable with touching. There were frequent "whole group back rubs" in which everyone sat in a tight circle and massaged the shoulders of the person ahead of them. There was dancing and flirting. The tingle of sexual attraction was everywhere. And there was a sense of respect for those whose body language said that they felt a little more hesitant about all of this.

There was a healthy testing of limits, too, always a challenge to adult leaders-and also an important sign of youthful aliveness and autonomy. A few individuals needed to be called back to the group's ground rules to respect each other by listening. One small group, instead of working on the given task, tested their account-ability to the larger group and to me by holding personal conversations and leaving undone the task we were working on. But their active dissent was never very disruptive. When they needed space to process work or just to play, they used the universal adolescent technique for "psyching out" adults: their faces took on weary, bored expressions. A mere half hour later after break with lots of junk food, they wore energetic faces.

These teens made time for shared expressions of their faith, and for individual expressions. In both efforts the teens were intentional about "being real." This group was encouraged to question, explore and affirm spirituality using language that was meaningful to them. Some of them took their faith energies into the realm of social concerns: they wanted to do something about racism in their own homes and towns, and openly shared painful experiences about it. Others could not relate such concerns to faith, being concerned instead with issues like getting along with siblings.

I watched some teens struggle with their need to be just like the group and their need to take a stand as an individual. I saw the hurt on one young woman's face when, after her vulnerable disclosure, someone in the group laughed. And I watched from the side after that session was over as that person painfully apologized to her.

It was not a "perfect" group. But these teens provided me with a wonderful opportunity to observe healthy adolescent spirituality (different from perfection) in action. There is a diversity to adolescent spirituality that resists categorization. Any description of healthy adolescent spirituality will be invalid for someone. Despite the unique, strongly individual qualities of spirituality, however, it can be considered in light of some of the following common features.

## Common Features of Healthy Adolescent Spirituality

Healthy adolescent spirituality has a "wholism" about it, a refusal to separate itself from the rest of the teen's being. It includes positive attitudes about the body, sexuality, intellectual and mental well-being. Antiquated notions that "play" is somehow anti-spiritual find no room in the expression of healthy adolescent spirituality. Laughter, spontaneity, lightness, play, and enjoyment are primary spiritual expressions/activities. So are moments of quiet reflection. It is not only the times when the young person prays, worships, or displays those personal qualities (virtues) traditionally related to spirituality. The person as a whole is the bearer of spirituality.

Healthy adolescent spirituality is characterized by a basic sense of self-acceptance. In the midst of the search for identity, a healthy spirituality supports the young person's identity struggles, with its affirmation of a higher source of valuing that accepts the teen in unconditional regard.

Healthy spirituality enables teens to accept and deal with their failures, including those times when they do not live up to their own moral standards. Healthy adolescent spirituality contains room for accepting the "negative" aspects of one's self, and mechanisms for self-forgiveness. Twelve Step-based recovery programs describe this process of self-acceptance and forgiveness with phrases such as "letting go" and "turning things over" to the care of a Higher Power. An environment that supports healthy adolescent spirituality invites young people to active rather than passive formation/clarification of values, and encourages them to wrestle with value conflicts.

Healthy adolescent spirituality is lived out in a positive and supportive peer group. It would be silly to expect teens, who are peer-centered, not to express their spirituality in a peer group. A peer group provides the setting for the kind of role experimentation so crucial to teen development. It is a place where a young person can take risks or try out new ideas. But it is also a kind of "experiential laboratory" for youth to learn about the connections between their relationships with people and their relationship to God/Higher Power. "I believe that God works through people" many an adolescent affirms in treatment. In homes and schools, other teens may not have such a precise and focused language to describe where they encounter the transcendent in life. But they know there often is a "transpersonal" quality to their friendships and peer relationships—an awareness of something happening beyond the person to person encounter.

As a laboratory for adolescent spirituality, the peer group also becomes a place where teens shape commitments to one another and to higher values. Doing so means that teens will also encounter the need to forgive others when commitments are broken and values trespassed. Healthy adolescent spirituality supports young people to do the hard work of seeking and offering forgiveness in a community, where friends betray friends despite good intentions and where feelings of hurt or rejection are possible along with those of support and inclusion.

But the peer-centered quality of the adolescent years does not exclude individual and personal spaces in the spiritual life of the teen. In fact, healthy adolescent spirituality balances individual autonomy and community. It maintains the creative tension between independence and connection in the form of increasingly mutual interdependency among persons. Diversity is encouraged and acknowledged. There are ways to work through the conflict that comes from diversity. Adolescent spirituality has both a private and public dimension: it is simultaneously an individual and community experience.

An environment of healthy adolescent spirituality includes adults. There is an inter-generational quality that balances the focus of being with the peer group. Adults do not abandon teens to "do their own thing" apart from adult participation in their lives. Instead, adults offer themselves as resources, supporters, limit-setters, and guides for teens who need an adult presence in their lives. A healthy environment for nurturing adolescent spiritual growth includes someplace for the young person to call "home." It may or may not be a traditional family dwelling, but it is a place where the young person can belong, and yet can also achieve some differentiation from others who dwell there.

Healthy adolescent spirituality creates and utilizes "rituals" to celebrate landmark events and passages, to mark entries and departures, and to give symbolic expression to the young person's world. Ritual is a reliable patterned use of symbol. The habit of sitting in the same chair at the dinner table is a ritual of sorts, a pattern of behavior that helps organize reality. Healthy teen spirituality uses rituals, not as empty forms to be mindlessly performed, but as living, vibrant expressions of meaning. Some organized groups of teenagers begin their time together by singing. Others, like Twelve Step groups, employ rituals of introduction that allow everyone to be included, especially newcomers. Often teens who gather in casual friendship groups will inadvertently establish a pattern of "checking in" with each other about the events of the day before going on to the day's activity. The traditions and patterns surrounding celebration of a "golden birthday" or other age-marker events such as acquiring a driver's license find some level of ritual expression where a healthy spirituality is encouraged. And there are symbolic ways to acknowledge closure and loss as they occur in the lives of youth.

Healthy adolescent spirituality actively engages the world. It is not a once-a-week, only-when-I'm-thinking-about-God kind of experience. It calls for action and response, instead of stagnant separation. If offers a safe time to practice taking on increased responsibility. Some of the activity of adolescent spirituality may be focused in social action, as young people translate their developmental idealism into a desire to make the world better. Some of the activity occurs in living out values, as spirituality shapes the young person's way of treating other people.

There exists in healthy adolescent faith an openness to doubt and the encouragement of questioning, exploration, inquiry and growth. An environment of healthy spirituality supports and equips youth to use their intellectual abilities in their faith exploration. It encourages expression of emotion and feeling rather than repression. Such an environment respects the use of past tradition as a resource for faith, without elevating it.

Healthy adolescent spirituality acknowledges the sometimes uncomfortable restlessness of the human search for wholeness. It also recognizes the reality of negative, uncreative suffering (sickness, trauma, or abuse) that many persons experience. That is, it honors the constructive role of struggle, without glorifying pain and suffering. Adolescent spirituality combines understandings of why suffering exists with emerging moral concerns for justice. In a healthy spirituality, young people find assistance and encouragement to deal with the grey areas of such questions, instead of being pressured to adopt "black or white" reasoning.

People are allowed to have bad days. Pain can be acknowledged along with happiness. Difficult feelings and experiences are not glossed over with messages of false cheer. In healthy expressions of adolescent spirituality, there is room and encouragement to "be real."

Finally, healthy adolescent spirituality includes awareness of and an appreciation for that which is beyond ordinary knowledge. It seeks "updated" images and metaphors for persons to both describe and relate to this "Higher Power." It allows teens to reflect critically on the values, symbols, and assumptions inherited from one's family or community. It is "peeking around the corner" into the young adult years, toward a time when identity is less dependent upon other people, and when authority is vested in that internalized self—a "self-authorization"—rather than in the actual external or internalized voices of others. Adolescent spiritually looks toward these aspects of faith which become realized in young adulthood and beyond.

## Helping Healthy Spirituality To Happen

If spirituality were simply a matter of "having it" or "not having it," then the only way concerned adults could encourage healthy spirituality in teens would be to pour in some content called "spiritual"—as if the teen were an empty container waiting to be filled! Fortunately, by understanding spirituality as a dynamic, developmental process, images emerge of how adults can support the formation of healthy adolescent spirituality.

Adolescent faith is a play or drama in process. Some acts are light, while others are heavy; some scenes involve multiple actors, while others employ soliloguy. This drama is simultaneously *a story about* real life, and life itself happening here and now. It requires immense efforts on the part of the actors to make the play happen. And yet the actors are aware that the play happens not only through their efforts, but also through the working of some off-stage, unseen power. The drama, not yet finished, may change or take unexpected turns in the next scene. No one watching can be certain how it will turn out. But there is a sense of hopeful expectation toward which it seems to move.

All images have their limitations, including this one. But I am using the play as one way to picture how adults can help to nurture healthy adolescent spiritual development. The metaphor of teen spirituality as a drama-in-process suggests that at any point along the way, it is still possible to add some new element to the set, or bring in a new character, or help someone find some new and different lines to speak—all in support of the story's unfolding. Adults who care about teens can actively support their spiritual development.

How can adults support healthy adolescent spiritual development? The material offered previously from the Search Institute study suggests some ways that parents, other adults, and community resources can work together to minimize the likelihood of a young person getting into trouble. The factors mentioned in the Search Institute Study point to how adults can support spiritual development as well, because the development of healthy adolescent spirituality takes place in environments which support the whole person's development. By "building into" the teens' lives the presence of non-parental adults who can be resources for them (coaches, youth-friendly church members, parents of friends) teens are less likely to engage in high-risk behaviors. And the availability of those adults helps maintain a relational network of support for the teen that contributes to faith development. What supports adolescent development will also support their faith development.

But there also are some unique aspects of spiritual development that are not captured in such broad brush strokes.

1. Adults support spiritual development of teens when they model faith for them. By modeling an open, searching, and wholistic faith for youths, adults assist young people to be open, searching, and wholistic as they grow in their spirituality.

2. Adults support spiritual development of teens when they provide stability while teens explore, experiment and change in their faith. Constancy without rigidity creates a "safety net" for the young person's explorations, allowing them to seek

out ideas and practices in contrast to those with which they are familiar. Such explorations allow youth to better discover and define their own perspectives. "I never thought very much about what I believed before. Going to my friend's church opened my eyes. I thought everybody did things just like we do. They did a lot of things that made me feel like God was some scary, far-away person. That's not what I believe about God, but I didn't know how much it mattered to me before." The young woman voicing these thoughts was helped to clarify her own understandings through the experience of another church whose perspectives contrasted with her own.

3. Adults can support healthy adolescent spirituality by expressing their faith as a family in whatever ways are most natural and appropriate. The family might mean a teenager and a single parent. Or it could mean a blended family, a more traditional two-parent family, or an extended family network. But whatever defines the parameters of family, when adults lead the way for faith expression teens have a clear family setting of spirituality both to embrace and to struggle against.

A young friend of mine who recently graduated from high school is part of a family whose members go together to an Al-Anon club each week. Another teen in aftercare (following chemical dependency treatment) said, "My dad is not the religious type and neither am I. But since I got home from treatment, he's been making an effort to sit down and have dinner with me. We usually read something from one of our meditation books right before we eat which is kinda cool because it's my dad, ya know, and I never did anything like that with him before."

A third young person describes her family's "weekly family meeting" on Sunday nights: "We talk about how the week has gone. If anyone has a problem with something another person in the family did, they can bring it up. Sometimes I don't feel like bringing it up, but I know if I need to I can. We also talk about what's going to happen in school the next week." Her family meeting takes place after the two teenagers in the family come home from their church youth group. Often the family meeting is also a place for discussion of church events.

There are also informal ways adults support faith development of teens through the family's expression of spirituality. One such way is the everyday living and communicating of family values. I am impressed when I encounter teens who are able to identify some of the values that are most important in their families. "My mom has a big value for education" reported a fifteen-year-old girl. "I guess it's a family value, 'cause we all try to make good grades in school." I asked if she knew that education was an important value in the family because her mother had told her so. "No, she never told me. We never talked about it. But you can tell. For one thing she's always reading some book. And she goes to all our school conferences. She asks lots of questions about our homework—I don't like that very much. It's kinda embarrassing that she knows all my teachers. Not really embarrassing. Just, like, I know it means school and education are important to her." Her mother never had to say "education is one of our strong family values." She expressed it in the way she and her family lived, and through her involvement with her teenagers' educations. Sometimes expressing faith as a family happens in the everyday living out of values and commitments.

## Healthy Adolescent Spirituality
## and the Discussion of Adolescent Satanism

Occasionally I encounter adults or young people who want to know why I do not consider adolescent satanism a healthy expression of spirituality. I have discussed in this chapter some of the features that are essential to a healthy adolescent spirituality, and some of the ways that adults can support young people in their spiritual development. My conclusions about both of these areas assume a partnership between young people and adults. Regardless of how "benign" its form, adolescent satanism never leads to partnership or mutuality. For a spirituality to be healthy, it must acknowledge and affirm the inter-dependence of persons. Also it must go beyond interpersonal partnerships to concern for the earth, its human inhabitants, and the rest of earth's creatures. Adolescent satanism lacks any concern for people (other than the self), for animals (evident in their barbaric treatment of them), or the earth.

Young people and adults exist in a state of interdependency with one another. Each needs the other. I have written about some of the ways young people need adults, and some of the functions adults provide that are most helpful to teens. It is easy to forget that adults need teens, too.

Adults need adolescents who will call us to live up to the values we hope to teach them and the commitments we make. Adults need teens who expect us to participate in healing the world's ills. Their heightened sense of idealism and energy are much needed by us. Without them, we become complacent, content with the status quo, or just plain lazy. Adults need teens who will challenge our rules, our authority, our materialism, even our carefully managed images of ourselves. Otherwise we will become rigid, boring, or too sure of ourselves. Adults need teens who can embody all the joy and excitement, the hurt and chaos, and the hunger for the future that is part of our mutual humanity.

Healthy adolescent spirituality happens in partnership. Adolescent satanism recognizes no partners. Healthy adolescent spirituality grows and develops—it is "going somewhere." Adolescent satanism does not grow, nor does it invite its participants to grow. Adolescent satanism focuses upon opposition and destruction. Satanism negates, while healthy adolescent spirituality affirms. It affirms life with all its ups and downs, and young people amidst all their celebrations, failures and searchings.

### The Last Word: Teen Perspective on Spirituality

What is spirituality as defined by teens themselves? The quotations at the beginning of this chapter come from teens in a chemical dependency aftercare program. When asked to talk about what "spiritual" means to them, their comments were enlightening. "I used to think it was talking about God, praying and stuff. Now I think it is more about what I do with my life every day. I mean, that can include praying. But the important thing is how I live." This young man is in the process of redefining spirituality away from overtly "God-related" activities such as prayer, and toward seeing his way of living as a God-related activity. Another quips, "Spirituality is believing in something without having to be religious."

Here are some other insights:

"When I really love somebody and we support each other, it's spiritual."

"Just sitting quietly in church is when I feel closest to God. I try to shut my thoughts off and listen to the quiet."

"Spirituality to me means knowing there's a Higher Power working to help me out. I mean, there's a lot that I need help with! Some days you know it more than others, that something out there cares about you."

"It's spiritual when we do things to help the earth. At our school we recycle paper and cans. Now my family recycles too. When we took a vacation to the Rocky Mountains, I felt this connection with the environment."

"Spiritual means feeling peaceful, like when I fall asleep with my puppy curled up beside me."

Their responses point to the breadth of adolescents' perspectives on spirituality. One sees it in terms of some ineffable expression of a yet undiscovered purpose in life, while another senses it in the experience of intimate friendships. Still another relates spirituality to music, while a fourth understands it to be about beliefs and the lifelong process of searching.

What seems to be missing here is any sense that young people, by virtue of their youth, are "anti-spiritual." If we translate the desires of young people to stand apart from the faith of their elders as a desire to stand apart from faith, we severely misread the evidence. Young people are not inherently anti-spiritual. But they are in search of an expression of spirituality that makes sense to them, has meaning for them, and can be claimed as their own.

There is a freshness and an honesty in these comments by which young people attempt to give words and meaning to their experience of what constitutes spirituality.

That is a sign of great hope.

# About The Author

Joyce Mercer is a minister in the Presbyterian Church U.S.A. She is also a graduate of Yale Divinity School, the McCormick Theological Seminary in Chicago, Illinois, and a Fellow in the College of Chaplains. In addition to her ministerial work, Joyce has received a M.S.W. from the University of Connecticut. She is also a licensed independent clinical social worker in the state of Minnesota.

Before becoming a pastor of Mayflower United Church of Christ in Minneapolis, Minnesota, Joyce served as chaplain in an adolescent chemical dependency program. Joyce frequently lectures on topics as varied as satanism, family dynamics, faith and health issues, and adolescent development. She has also conducted workshops for the Women's Chemical Dependency Center on the topic of adolescent girls and father loss, and consults with halfways houses for chemically dependent teens.

# *Works Cited*
## Chapter 1

1. (p. 1) Anton Szandor LaVey, *The Satanic Bible,* (New York: Avon Books, 1969), p. 23 - 24.

2. (p. 3) For a concise and objective summary of the Church of Satan, see its entry in *The Encyclopedia of American Religions,* J. Gordon Melton (Detroit, MI: Gale Research Co., 1987).

3. (p. 4) From the July - August 1972 edition of the Church of Satan's publication, *The Cloven Hoof,* as reported by Randall H. Alfred in his chapter of *The New Religious Consciousness,* Charles Y. Glock and Robert Bellah, eds. (Berkeley, CA: University of California Press, 1976), p. 185.

4. (p. 4) Anton Szandor LaVey, *The Satanic Bible,* (New York: Avon Books, 1969), p. 44.

5. (p. 6) Anton Szandor LaVey, *The Satanic Bible,* (New York: Avon Books, 1969), p. 25.

6. (p. 7) Anton Szandor LaVey, *The Satanic Bible,* (New York: Avon Books, 1969), p. 134 - 135.

7. (p. 8) Randall H. Alfred in his chapter of *The New Religious Consciousness,* Charles Y. Glock and Robert Bellah, eds. (Berkeley, CA: University of California Press, 1976), p. 188, a footnote to a description of hedonism as one of the attractions of satanism to its members.

8. (p. 8) Anton Szandor LaVey, *The Satanic Bible,* (New York: Avon Books, 1969), p. 110.

9. (p. 8) Anton Szandor LaVey, *The Satanic Bible,* (New York: Avon Books, 1969), p. 114.

10. (p. 8) Anton Szandor LaVey, *The Satanic Bible,* (New York: Avon Books, 1969), p. 115.

11. (p. 10) *"Apostle of Darkness",* and *"Satan's disciple leads a defiant, lonely life",* by Lisa Davis in the Religion Section of the *Arizona Republic,* Saturday, May 19, 1990.

12. (p. 12) J. Gordon Melton, *The Encyclopedic Handbook of Cults in America* (New York: Garland, 1986), p. 250.

## Chapter 2

1. (p. 30) Michelle Smith, *Michelle Remembers* (New York: Congdon & Lattes, 1980, Distributed by—New York: St. Martins Press).

2. (p. 36) James Fowler, *Stages of Faith: The Psychology of Human Development and the Quest for Meaning* (San Francisco: Harper and Row, 1981), p. 14.
3. (p. 36) I borrow this phrase from educator, Sara Little, and from James Fowler who also uses it in his afore-mentioned discussion/definition of faith. It seems to me to be a helpful description of the nature of faith as a deep-felt and personal attachment, not merely an external fascination with a figure.

## Chapter 3

1. (p. 43) Daniel Stern, *The First Relationship: Infant and Mother* from "The Developing Child" series, ed. by Jerome Bruner, Michael Cole and Barbara Lloyd (Cambridge, MA: Harvard University Press, 1977), p. 33.
2. (p. 45) Margaret Mahler, Fred Pine, and Anni Bergman, *The Psychological Birth of the Human Infant: Symbiosis and Individuation* (New York: Basic Books), 1975.
3. (p. 46) This phrase is borrowed from the title of Louise Kaplan's excellent book, *Adolescence: The Farewell to Childhood* (New York: Simon and Schuster, 1984).
4. (p. 57) See Merton P. Strommen and A. Irene Strommen, *Five Cries of Parents* (San Francisco: Harper and Row)1985 for a helpful discussion of the experience of adolescence from the parents' perspective.

## Chapter 4

1. (p. 61) Anton Szandor LaVey, *The Satanic Bible,* (New York: Avon Books, 1969), p. 34.
2. (p. 62) *The Holy Bible, (New Revised Standard Version),* (New York: Oxford Press; Division of Christian Education of the National Council of the Churches of Christ in the United States of America), 1989.
3. (p. 63) Anton Szandor LaVey, *The Satanic Bible,* (New York: Avon Books, 1969),p. 87 - 90.
4. (p. 69) Anton Szandor LaVey, *The Satanic Bible,* (New York: Avon Books, 1969), p. 117.
5. (p. 72) Comments from a telephone conversation on October 1, 1990 with J. Gordon Melton at the Institute for the Study of American Religions, Santa Barbara, CA.
6. (p. 78) Anton Szandor LaVey, *The Satanic Bible,* (New York: Avon Books, 1969), p. 149.

7. (p. 78) Anton Szandor LaVey, *The Satanic Bible,* (New York: Avon Books, 1969), p. 33.

8. (p. 88) J. Gordon Melton, *Encyclopedic Handbook of Cults in America,* (New York: Garland Press, 1986), p. 78.

## Chapter 5

1. (p. 92) *The Holy Bible, (New Revised Standard Version),* (New York: Oxford Press; Division of Christian Education of the National Council of the Churches of Christ in the United States of America), 1989.

2. See note 1.

3. See note 1.

4. See note 1.

5. See note 1.

6. (p. 94) I am indebted to two resources for helping me wade through the vast amounts of extra Biblical material and ancient sources about Satan as a fallen angel. Primary is the work of Jeffrey Burton, *The Devil: Perceptions of Evil from Antiquity to Primitive Christianity,* (Ithaca, NY: Cornell University Press), 1977. I draw heavily upon his summary of the pseudepigraphal materials for my understanding. See also *The Interpreters Dictionary of the Bible,* (Nashville, TN: Abingdon Press), 1962. See the entry "Devil" in Volume A - D. Also see James H. Charlesworth, ed. *The Old Testament: Pseudepigrapha* (Garden City: Doubleday), 1983.

7. (p. 100) As noted by Peter A. Olsson, "Adolescent Involvement with the Supernatural and Cults: Or New Bottles for Old Wine", in *Psychodynamic Perspectives on Religion, Sect and Cult,* ed. by David A. Halpern (Boston: John Wright Press, 1983), p. 250.

8. (p. 100) As noted by Peter A. Olsson, "Adolescent Involvement with the Supernatural and Cults: Or New Bottles for Old Wine", in *Psychodynamic Perspectives on Religion, Sect and Cult,* ed. by David A. Halpern (Boston: John Wright Press, 1983), p. 247.

## Chapter 6

1. (p. 114) From Search Institute Source: A quarterly information resource on issues facing children, adolescents, and families, December 1990, Volume VI, Number 3, p. 1-2. Used with permission.

## Chapter 7

1. (p. 125) James Fowler, *Stages of Faith: The Psychology of Human Development and the Quest for Meaning* (San Francisco: Harper and Row, 1981), p. 16. Ken Stokes takes this phrase, "Faith Is a Verb", as the title of this very readable and helpful exploration of "faithing", the active experience of faith as a process for persons.

2. (p. 129) Fowler's work relies on the developmental theories of Piaget, Kohlberg, and Erikson. In recent years these theories have been strongly critiqued by researchers such as Carol Gilligan of Harvard, for their failure to take into account the differences between women's and men's developmental processes. Fowler's more recent writings address these issues.